Explication

COMMUNICATION CONCEPTS

This series reviews enduring concepts that have guided scholarly inquiry in communication, including their intellectual evolution and their uses in current research. Each book is designed to provide organized background reading for those who intend further study of the subject.

EDITOR

Steven H. Chaffee, *Stanford University*

ASSOCIATE EDITORS

Charles R. Berger, *University of California, Davis*
Joseph N. Cappella, *University of Pennsylvania*
Robert P. Hawkins, *University of Wisconsin-Madison*
Mark R. Levy, *University of Maryland, College Park*
Neil M. Malamuth, *University of California, Los Angeles*
Jack McLeod, *University of Wisconsin-Madison*
Peter Monge, *University of Southern California*
Byron Reeves, *Stanford University*
Michael Schudson, *University of California, San Diego*
Ellen Wartella, *University of Illinois at Urbana-Champaign*

EDITORIAL ASSISTANT

Caroline Schooler, *Stanford University*

Explication

Steven H. Chaffee

SAGE PUBLICATIONS
The International Professional Publishers
Newbury Park   London   New Delhi

For information address:

SAGE Publications, Inc.
2455 Teller Road
Newbury Park, California 91320

SAGE Publications Ltd.
6 Bonhill Street
London EC2A 4PU
United Kingdom

SAGE Publications India Pvt. Ltd.
M-32 Market
Greater Kailash I
New Delhi 110 048 India

Printed in the United States of America

ISBN 0-8039-4474-8 (c)   ISBN 0-8039-4475-6 (p)

ISSN 1057-7440

FIRST PRINTING, 1991

Sage Production Editor: Astrid Virding

Citation Instructions:

When citing a **Communications Concepts** issue, please follow this reference style:

Chaffee, Steven H. (1991). *Communication Concepts 1: Explication.* Newbury Park, CA: Sage.

Contents

Foreword

This is the first volume in a series devoted to concepts in the study of communication. While each volume that follows will be devoted to a particular concept, this book is concerned with the process of conceptualizing itself. And while other books in this series will be prefaced by an Editor's Introduction, this Foreword will serve that purpose here—as well as introduce the series as a whole.

Making a concept explicit is, in a broad sense, a purpose of all discourses on communication concepts. The purpose of this volume on explication is to formulate some of the common principles that guide this practice as it is followed by many communication researchers.

Each scholar, myself included, has a somewhat specialized view of explication and what it helps us accomplish. Among those who have read and commented on earlier drafts of this book are Charles Berger, Glen Broom, Richard Carter, Robert Davis, Jose Gaztambide-Geigel, Dennis Kinsey, Hye-Ryeon Lee, Debra Lieberman, Matthew Lombard, Jack McLeod, Geetu Melwani, Peter Monge, Clifford Nass, Zhongdang Pan, Byron Reeves, David Ritchie, Donald Roberts, Caroline Schooler, Pamela Shoemaker, and Valerie Sue. Unfortunately, I cannot hold any of my helpful colleagues responsible for errors that remain despite their best efforts to improve what I've said.

Explication is an intellectual process to be applied to any concept one intends to make the focus of planned research, or to discuss seriously. Much will also be said here about communication, through examples of conceptual aspects of research with which I have been associated. Examples could as easily have been found in other areas of communication research. The field is growing rapidly, and my hope that this book will prove useful extends to all branches of communication inquiry.

The intended audience is people who plan to study communication, especially in the empirical tradition, and those who need to understand how that tradition of scholarship works. This includes those who, in their expository writing, discuss communication concepts; critics of empirical approaches; and students who want to acquire an understanding of the academic literature of this field. Much of the content here is introductory, but it is hoped that the experienced scholar too will find new ideas, and clarification of old ones, in these pages. The same hope extends to the other volumes that will follow in this series.

The material in this book comes from many sources, collected over some three decades of studying and teaching communication research. My intellectual debts are too numerous to detail; certainly the references in the text to particular published sources are wholly inadequate to this purpose. The subject matter here overlaps both communication theory and research methods, and is best read in conjunction with textbooks and other materials on those subjects. I have tried not to duplicate what is readily available elsewhere.

One feature of this series is that each volume in it is to be brief—short enough to be used both by students as an introduction to a subject and by researchers for easy reference. Hence this book condenses much that is philosophically ponderable and pragmatically arguable, glossing over entire bodies of important literature so it can get on with its own central task. Trusting that others will readily provide them, it arrives unadorned by the usual academic qualifications, caveats, and cavils.

—Steven H. Chaffee, *Series Editor*

EXPLICATION

STEVEN H. CHAFFEE

1. Concept Explication: An Overview

This book is about a way of thinking. It is concerned with the disciplined use of words, with observation of human behavior, and especially with the connection between the two. Communication research mostly takes the form of words, although it is often presented through numerical entries in tables and graphs as well. But numbers and words are of little interest unless they can be translated back into conceptual terms. Those concepts are our way of organizing and clarifying what we observe.

An instance of communication is not, in its entirety, observed directly. Some aspects are always imagined, by the participants and by anyone attempting to study communication. When we think about communication we use concepts, in verbal form to represent what we observe and imagine; these conceptual terms, from which we build theories, carry meanings. Without conceptual definition, the words we use to describe and discuss communication are mere words—no improvement over mere numbers.

Many components of the communication process can be experienced directly, such as the words we say or read, and some of the reactions we and others have to them. These real-life perceptions provide the occasion, and the raw data, for our theorizing about communication. Concepts establish the linkage between communication perceptions, which everyone has, and theories, which communication scientists and critics build and test. Everyone has at least implicit theories about communication; we could not function very well in life without them. But often what we imagine fails to match what we experience in our own communication. Sometimes labeled "a failure to communicate," this problem might more properly be seen as a failure of our theories.

My purpose here is to improve the quality of conceptualization by scholars who undertake to study human communication formally. Concept explication can strengthen the ties among theory, observation, and research. To the extent that it helps other educated people sharpen their tools for thinking, even if they are not themselves communication scientists, this book will have succeeded beyond its particular purposes. Although improved understanding of communication, either by researchers or by people in general, is not the immediate goal here, it too would be a welcome by-product.

"Things Are Not as They Seem"

Twentieth-century social and behavioral science, of which communication is a fairly recent branch (Schramm, 1963), grows out of a loose assumption about the relationship between science and society. Two of the best-known exponents of this view were Karl Marx and Sigmund Freud. Their research has largely passed from active science into the literary canon, but the implicit philosophical message they popularized remains: "Things are not as they seem."

There are underlying causes of social and behavioral phenomena, but according to this assumption, they are not to be understood by observing the surface of human events. What we think we see happening in everyday experience is actually a result of unseen forces. For example, Marx pointed out the realities of society in the Industrial Revolution, in ways that were not easily recognizable in a worker's daily life. Freud searched for explanations of both ordinary and bizarre behavior deep in the unconscious. To formulate these explanations, Marx and Freud invented new concepts, such as their definitions of *class struggle* and *capital*, *ego* and *id*, respectively. Many of their best-remembered writings concern the meanings of these ideas, and their relationships with other ideas in elaborate conceptual schemes.

These intellectual giants were also dogged empiricists. Marx (1867) devoted many pages to analyses based on statistical reports of the British royal commissions on the new industrial working class. Freud spent many of his working hours interviewing clinical patients according to new protocols he had developed. These methods—statistical interpretation, clinical interrogation—remain among the standard tools of the social and behavioral sciences today. The methods, though, are not scientific unless they are used in the service of a theory, to pursue a conception of things as they "really" are rather than as they might seem on the surface of one's casual experience. Marx and Freud had very strong theories about unseen processes, and that was the central reason for their introducing new concepts.

Communication research provides latter-day examples of both kinds of thinking. Tichenor, Donohue, and Olien (1970) took a page from Marx by conceiving of the "knowledge gap" that results when a public information campaign succeeds in informing some people—but at the cost of exacerbating the disparities in knowledge between society's haves and have-nots. Schramm (1949) relied on Freud's dualism of *the reality principle* and *the pleasure principle* in deriving a typology of mass media use (see also Schramm, Lyle, & Parker, 1961).

It is not to the scientific methods nor even the particular theories of Marx or Freud, though, that today's communication scientist owes the greatest debt. It is to their more general working assumption that we must look beneath the surface of life as we normally experience it, beyond our personal perceptions, to comprehend "what is really going on." McLuhan (1964) is among those who have pursued this assumption in mass media studies, with his contention that television has restored Western thought to a pattern of simultaneity after centuries of linear thinking patterns due to the dominance of print media.

Communication practitioners, philosophers, and scientists alike think and write a great deal about the manifest world of communication. What sets the scientist apart is the formal conceptualization of processes that are not obvious, coupled with a determination to bring them into view in an equally formal manner. Analytic description, classification, and criticism of communication institutions and products are all worthy forms of intellectual effort, but this volume is directed especially toward those who take a scientific approach, in a broad sense of that term.

Observation: The Empirical Base

Research on human communication demands a lot of work in the creation and collection of data. To say that this is an empirical field of study means that it is based on the plentiful evidence we observe in the real world. The student of communication spends a great deal of time observing human events—people sending one another messages, mostly. But we would never learn very much about communication by simply observing what goes on around us. Communication scholars go to great effort to gather evidence that would not ordinarily enter their lives. One can find, somewhere, on practically any given day, a student of human communication engaged in such otherwise odd behaviors as the following:

— reading through very old newspapers, and keeping a careful record of the occurrence of certain kinds of statements;
— hiding behind a one-way mirror, watching children watch television;
— editing a video presentation that incorporates material from several different sources, to be shown in an experimental laboratory to college students;
— calling telephone numbers, selected randomly, and asking the adult who has had the most recent birthday what he or she thinks about current issues in the news;
— sitting in the corner of a meeting room, making notes on who says what to whom while a group of people at the table tries to solve a problem it will never encounter again.

These might be judged as strange behavior patterns, in and of themselves. Explication is the intellectual process that links such activities to broader propositions about communication. These and thousands of other examples of research work are undertaken because each is thought of as an *operational definition*. That is, they all entail operations on the day-to-day world, painstakingly arranged by the investigator because of an explication that connects them with a concept. An operational definition is often not of much interest in and of itself. Most of our propositions about communication are statements about general concepts, but empirical research can only be about operational definitions. Explication, then, consists of the thinking that relates

theory with research. All research is in this sense *qualitative*, regardless of whether it is *quantitative*.

Most communication researchers devote a large portion of
their time to activities whose import lies in an operational definition of a larger concept. Coding content, running subjects in
an experiment, and interviewing respondents in a survey are
time-consuming forms of work. Whether they are worth the
effort put into them depends on the quality of thought that
has gone into the concept's explication. A thousand hours
spent coding utterances of husbands on TV, or measuring the
pulse rates of sophomores who are being shown an erotic film,
or asking people how they plan to vote, may be time wasted if
the resultant data do not serve a conceptual purpose. Explication, then, can save hours and deserves some investment of
time itself.

This is not to say that communication can or should be entirely
an empirical field. No science relies solely on what is readily observable. We must begin any attempt to study human communication with the understanding that much of it lies beyond direct
human observation, even though it may be only imagined. Communication involves mental events that are very difficult to observe. We surely cannot see someone else think, and it is not
much easier to observe our own communication experience as individuals—much less as part of a larger society.

Any operational procedure falls far short of observation of the
whole process of any rich communication phenomenon. By scientific norms, our evidence has an inherent make-do quality, although we continue trying to improve on operational methods.
The more fundamental critique of communication research is to
be lodged at the conceptual level, by working out the relations
between the meanings of concepts, not just the relations between
empirical variables. Our measures will be improved more by
evaluation of what they are intended to measure then by technical tinkering. Explication should tell us, among other things, the
extent to which we are falling short of studying what we really
intend.

The process of explication embraces both the conceptual world
and the real world, crossing those lines repeatedly as the student
attempts to improve conceptualization through research. This

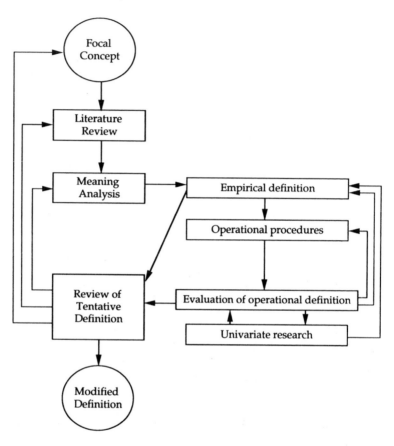

Figure 1.1. Concept Explication as an Iterative Process

ongoing dialectic between operational and conceptual scholarship (Blalock, 1982) cannot be overemphasized here. What follows is a series of steps, in a logical sequence, to which the
investigator can refer at various stages in a program of research
on a concept. This is not, however, a recipe through which one
proceeds step-by-step in the sense of the investigator "being
done" with one stage once he or she has moved on to the next.
Often research begins with a fuzzy idea or a topical term and
its conceptual development can never be considered complete.
The assiduous investigator can return to various points in this

outline from time to time, comparing evidence to ideas in an on-going process that will last as long as the concept continues to generate interest. This circularity of the explication process is di-agramed schematically in Figure 1.1. For some scholars this can last a lifetime; rarely does it end with the completion of a single study.

Primitive and Derived Terms

Conceptualization is built of words, and we must start some-where. In any conceptual scheme there are some *primitive terms,* which are accepted as commonly understood or as given (Hempel, 1952). The existence and acceptability of these concepts is assumed, which means they are not questioned within the framework of research built upon them. In other work, the prim-itive terms of an established tradition may very well be chal-lenged, though. A "paradigm shift" to a new scientific tradition (Kuhn, 1970) is often based upon rejection of one set of primitive terms and its replacement with a new set.

The primitive terms of communication research are not always the same. Most commonly, though, one essential given is the in-dividual, or person. While the conceptual or operational defini-tion of a human being might be quite controversial in, say, zoology or medical ethics, it is rarely a matter of much dispute in human communication research. To get on with our work, we need to assume that people exist and we know them when we see them.

Some branches of communication research assume as well the existence of supra-individual entities, such as families or organi-zations or societies. In some scholarly traditions these terms are defined by specifying what persons constitute the larger entity, but not always. It is possible to speak of television, for example, without reference to any individual or group of individuals. Philosophical disputes naturally arise in some research contexts over the meaning of such a term; at that point it has become too problematic to be a primitive.

Time, which is a primitive term in some sciences, is often treated that way in communication as well. We define people in relation to one another in time, often implicitly. For example, when we say that two people constitute a couple, we assume without thinking much about it that they have been communicating over some extended period. The assumption that we know what time means in this context is a convenience. We would be foolish to expend a lot of effort on its definition; it would then cease to be convenient—and no longer a primitive term. Still, there are situations in which we can benefit from conceptualizing time-related concepts (see Chapter 11).

A *derived term* is built of primitive terms. A couple, a group, a family, a community, and a society, are examples of derived terms. Each is made up of specifiable relations between persons. As a second example, if *word* is a primitive term, it is possible to define such entities as a sentence, a chapter, or a scene in terms of words.

Explication becomes important when concepts are being derived from primitive terms. Even seemingly simple statements relating persons to time, for example, may benefit from analysis. The concept of *college freshmen* refers to a particular set of persons, but only for a particular time (the freshman year). In a later time (next year) they will be replaced by an entirely different set of persons. The concept, though, will be unchanged. When time is invoked as part of an observation about an aggregate like this, quite different meanings can result. Consider, for example, the following statements: "College freshmen are becoming more liberal" and "College freshmen are becoming more conservative." Depending on the time frame of reference and whether it is meant to apply to one freshman or to the aggregate, each statement can be valid. The first is usually the case for *individual* students *during the freshman year;* most college students come from relatively conservative home backgrounds, and they become more liberal over time. But the second statement can also be true, at the *aggregate* level *across years;* during the Reagan-Bush Administration, for example, each succeeding group of freshmen held somewhat more conservative views than did the previous year's incoming class.

Mental events are also conceptualized in derived terms built on primitive terms. One mentalistic distinction common in research is that between *objects* and their *attributes*. Data are often organized as a series of objects on which several attributes have been observed. If the objects are persons, for example, their attributes might be gender, reticence, and self-esteem; if the objects are messages, then the observed attributes might include length, bias, and persuasiveness.

How are the terms *object* and *attribute* derived? Carter (1965) proposed that an object is "anything that exists psychologically for a person." This means that objects include not only rocks and other people, but also abstract notions: states, such as love; institutions, such as television; stages, such as childhood. Use of *object* as an empirical term would require not just the assertion that these ideas can exist psychologically, but also some showing that they do exist for the people being studied. This might be accomplished through content analysis of their statements, perhaps in response to open-ended questioning. A derived term is not a primitive; it requires evidence.

The concept of *attribute* is built, in turn, upon that of *object.* An object usually has a number of properties, or attributes, such as size or color, usefulness, dynamism, and so on. Research on human personality, for example, focuses on the collection of attributes that make up a particular type of individual. At the individualistic extreme, Allport (1955) suggests that personality researchers focus on the uniquely integrated configuration of attributes that explains "the 'Johnian' quality of John's behavior."

Carter (1965) points out, though, that attributes are also important in discriminating between objects. We evaluate objects in our environment in terms of their similarities and differences on specific attributes. We also communicate a lot about those discriminations, and we build up mutual understandings in this way. In discussing politics, one person may say, "I side with the Democrats on domestic policy, but with the Republicans on foreign policy." A second person may agree with this set of discriminations, even though the two of them support opposing parties, that is, one is a Democrat and the other a Republican. It is through comparison of two objects (e.g., parties) that the attributes become the basis of communication in this model.

Consumer researchers often analyze people's decision processes in terms of the attributes used in comparing brands (objects) in a product category (Jacoby, 1975). For instance, some people buy the cheapest brand they can find, others the most expensive. Still others try to decide which looks nicest, or to find out which one is most durable. Ray (1973) notes that people often make very casual decisions when there are few discriminations between alternatives. When voters do not see major policy differences between candidates, they may just go for the name with which they are most familiar. Similarly, consumers who might put a lot of effort into choosing between competing brands of stereo equipment may readily buy whatever brand of soap they have seen advertised most often.

This usage of *attribute* corresponds closely to the term *variable* in communication research. Variance, the defining characteristic of a variable, is central to much of quantitative research. If a concept does not vary, there are no comparisons to make, and no purpose for most kinds of statistical analysis. Still, non-variable concepts can be quite useful in theory building, both as the basis for developing variable concepts (Hage, 1972) and as a subject of research in their own right. Theories of homeostasis and equifinality in communication, such as "balance" models of attitudes (Heider, 1959) or the notion of functional equivalence in people's use of mass media (Parker, 1963), proceed from the observation of a state that remains constant even when conditions seem to be changing. A condition that remains stable even when it could, and perhaps should, change suggests to some theorists that it is of the highest importance.

The general point of this rather lengthy consideration of primitive terms is that we must begin by using some concepts that are not defined, so that we can define others. The terms noted here—person, object, time, and so on—are common but by no means universal in communication research. What is important is to recognize which terms we are assuming as primitive, and which other terms these enable us to explicate.

Validity

Validity is the governing criterion of communication research. When we use a concept in research, we are constantly concerned with the match between its meaning in relation to our other concepts, and its *operational definition* in a particular study. Explication is a method of keeping track of these two definitional activities together. Does the operational definition represent the concept as we have meant it at a more abstract level? The concept of *intelligence*, for example, is usually explicated as including verbal, quantitative, analytic, and other abilities; operationally it may be represented by an IQ test score. This score can be satisfactory for many purposes, but it does not represent all we might mean by *intelligence*. On the other hand, one might not even need a precise IQ score for some research uses. Hovland, Lumsdaine, and Sheffield (1949), for example, found that simply knowing the highest grade in school a person had completed would provide sufficient data to predict very different responses to contrasting versions of a propaganda film. They decided that the slight gain in validity to be derived from looking up everyone's intelligence test scores was not worth the extra effort.

Validity should not be equated with "truth." Disappointing as this may sound, the philosophical concept of truth is not a usable criterion for a communication scientist. A meaning can be assigned and an operational definition concocted that might seem a valid representation for one purpose, but not for another; the most that can be said of "truth" in this rather common circumstance is that it could be evaluated according to a limited set of premises. Many debates over what constitutes "true intelligence," for example, are arguments over the proper premises. Some teachers complain about intelligence testing because they want a measure of the capacity to comprehend new ways of thinking, rather than of the ability to learn established ways quickly.

Although we all should hope our conclusions are true, their evaluation is guided by validity judgments; only after much research has been completed does a statement come to be viewed in the scholarly community as true—a status very few communication theories are ever likely to reach. Even then, the truth value is to be found more in the degree of agreement among scholars, an intersubjective criterion, than in any ultimate reality. When an accepted "truth" is called into question, research should begin anew, renewing the search for validity. In any science, when a statement is accepted as true, it is not subjected to continued research.

The concept of *opinion leaders* may be an example of an idea whose time has come and gone. Early research on election campaign effects (Lazarsfeld, Berelson, & Gaudet, 1944) found that mass media influences were filtered to some extent through peers. This discovery led to a de-emphasis of mass communication for several decades, but today we see relatively little concern with opinion leaders in respect to the dominance of television in politics. These ups and downs do not mean that the concept of opinion leader is true or untrue; to say that it has been true in some instances (which is true) adds little. A valid conceptual purpose for these observations is needed, and *opinion leaders* no longer seems to fulfill that scholarly need.

MacCorquodale and Meehl (1948) proposed the term *intervening variable* to refer to a concept that has been validated through an extended program of research; earlier, when that same concept was mainly an idea without much surrounding evidence, its status would have been that of a *hypothetical construct,* implying lesser validity. While research is bringing a concept along from its introduction as a hypothetical construct to the empirical position of an intervening variable, its truth value does not change, but its validity in the eyes of the scholarly community does. As an example, Krugman (1965) suggested the hypothetical construct of *low involvement* to explain why television advertising works as well as it does. Several decades later the variable of involvement is routinely used as an intervening variable in persuasion studies of all sorts—although there remains considerable ambiguity over its meaning (Roser, 1990; Salmon, 1986).

It is not so hard to abandon truth as one's ideal in explication as it is in other aspects of theorizing. Most of us can accept the assumption that there is no one "true" operational definition for a concept, no observation or event that represents the more abstract concept more "truly" than others. An explication of a concept specifies the operations a scientist must perform to produce an instance of the concept; validity is the general criterion by which we assess the adequacy of that operationalization once we have established our explication. A unit of measurement may be valid for one scholar's purposes but not for another's. For example, in survey research on cultivation Gerbner, Gross, Morgan, and Signorielli (1980) measure exposure to television in units of hours; in laboratory experiments on brain wave activity, Reeves, Thorson, and Schleuder (1986) sometimes use units of a fraction of a second. Each metric seems valid for its specific purpose, but would be a foolish choice for the other purpose. (Both measures are "true" regardless of purpose.) Some procedures for validation are discussed in Chapter 10.

The relationship between validity and reliability is also confusing for some. Reliability is implied in validity, but they are not the same concept. Validity refers to the relationship between the conceptual definition and the operational definition, whereas reliability has to do with operational definitions. Formally, reliability consists of freedom of an operational definition from random error. Put a different way, unreliability consists of random error in a set of observations and measurement procedures; invalidity grows with unreliability, regardless of the other merits of a measure.

Put yet another way, all operational definitions are subject to two kinds of error, random and systematic, both of which threaten validity. To the extent that random error is controlled or minimized, an operational definition is deemed reliable; to the extent that it also avoids systematic error (constantly representing some other concept besides the one intended), the measure is valid. If a measure is not reliable enough to capture what we want to measure, there is no point in inquiring further into its validity, so we should think of reliability as a necessary condition for validity.

Reliability and validity are sometimes thought of as being pitted against one another in decisions regarding operationalization. A common example is the choice between open-ended and fixed alternative question formats in interviewing people. When we want to know about people's communication experiences, we may have to ask them. Should we ask highly specific questions, which improve reliability by cutting down on totally irrelevant responses? Or, in the interest of other aspects of validity, should we ask a very general question, with repeated non-directive probes, to find out as much as possible about what the person has to tell us? There is no general answer to this dilemma. The goal, after all, is to maximize all aspects of validity, including reliability. But when choices must be made, the place to find guidance is in the explication.

Only if there is a clear conceptual definition of what we wish to know about can we assess the validity of the answers elicited by any method. Validity is evaluated in terms of the explication, not in terms of the raw phenomenon of communication the interview might evoke. If we have established what we want to know about, the more reliable operationalization is of course preferable.

Validity is an inference, a tentative conclusion that is constantly evaluated by the researcher. It is not an unarguable fact, reducible to precise quantitative terms. When research is presented to the scholarly community, fresh conclusions about its validity will be made by the researcher's colleagues. The best defense of a researcher's work is constructed in advance, through explication.

Procedures and Queries in Explication

In communication research we use many words, many meanings, and many pieces of evidence. The connections are not often clear, and the purpose of explication is to make them as clear as we can at each stage in research. Without explication, our words are nothing more than words, and our data add nothing to them. Theory, or more exactly *theorizing*, consists of an interplay among ideas, evidence, and inference. This transaction is conducted mostly in verbal forms, such as propositions, observations, and conclusions. Observation, as Charles Darwin remarked, "must be for or against some view if it is to be of any service" (Selltiz, Jahoda, Deutsch, & Cook, 1964).

The steps outlined in Chapters 2 through 8 should be covered in an explication, although not always in the order given. It is often necessary to cycle back to preliminary phases, such as the literature search, after evaluating a concept at a more advanced stage. What is presented here can serve as a checklist for the researcher explicating a concept, but it is not a recipe that guarantees results. It is a way of organizing the ongoing dialectic between theorizing and research that is the essence of communication inquiry.

2. Focal Concept

Most researchers begin by focusing in a preliminary way on one interesting condition and giving it a tentative name. This becomes a starting place, the focal concept. One basic question to ask is whether the concept is a *variable*. (If not, could one or more variables be derived from it? Consult Hage, 1972, Ch. 1-2.) What we can study about a concept depends a great deal upon whether it is actually a variable. Consider television viewing. Americans spend so much time watching TV that we sometimes speak of a television addict. At the other extreme on the scale of TV use is the non-viewer. Neither TV addict or non-viewer is a variable, but the viewing scale on which they differ is; all three are concepts. A researcher might begin work by focusing on either TV addicts or non-viewers. Before long, either idea leads to the overall variable of television use.

Variables are essential to many kinds of research because most theories about communication are about relationships between variable concepts. Theories of communication effects, for example, often propose that an increase in some kind of communication produces a corresponding increase in some outcome that can be attributed to the communication. Correlational theories, such as those that associate two different kinds of communication with one another, require variance in each concept if the covariance is to be demonstrated. Lacking variance, we may still employ a concept, but not in this way. For example, either a kind of communication that is always present or one that is always absent may have effects, but they are not testable in terms of variance.

Planned Use

Once a focal concept has been identified, further key questions can be addressed: How will this concept be used in research? From the outset, a researcher should have some idea whether the concept is to be studied by itself, or in association with other concepts. If the latter, would he/she study its antecedent causes, its subsequent effects, or its mediating role? If it is a constant, is it to be studied in conjunction with variable concepts? The kind of variable the researcher needs depends to some extent upon the kind of theory he/she expects to involve it in.

Unit Definition

Empirical research is built upon observation of objects, each of which is treated as a unit. The units of discourse, of observation, and of data analysis should be the same if the research is to match the meaning intended. In quantitative research, the problem of unit definition is succinctly captured in the question, "What is one?" Common units in communication research include the individual, the dyad (pair of interacting persons), the message or part of a message or a series of messages, the community, the medium (e.g., newspaper), the network of interacting persons, and so forth.

Unit definition may seem simple at the outset, but in practice it is no easy matter to remain consistent. Newspaper consumer research, for example, generates data on reading (an attribute of an individual), subscription (an attribute of a household), penetration ratio (an attribute of a community), and street sales (an attribute of a newspaper). It is not easy to put these bodies of data on a common footing.

In studying families it is hard not to shift between attributes of the family as a unit and attributes of its individual members. For example, cohesion is an attribute of the family, while feeling hurt is an attribute of one family member at a time. One common inconsistency in communication research is the "ecological fallacy" of drawing psychological inferences about individuals from observing patterns in larger units such as communities. Somewhat the reverse problem is the treatment of individual observations as if, when added up, they represent some higher-order entity (e.g., public opinion polls).

Units of study, then, are themselves concepts in need of explication. We need to define what constitutes a group before we can define interaction within or between groups; we need to define television in the course of conceptualizing its audience. Relationships, such as interactions between people, or consumption of mass media by their audiences, are sometimes treated as objects in data analysis, sometimes not. The main point for the moment is that unit definition is rarely straightforward or widely agreed upon; nor can one slip past the question by stipulating a simple assumption. As soon as a researcher begins either comparing or counting units, the issue of unit definition (and its relationship to the discourse in question) arises. This is the starting point of explication within empirical research.

Relationship to Time

Given the definition of a unit and the primitive assumption of time, two possibilities arise regarding variation. A variable in communication usually varies across units (e.g., persons) at a given time (*cross-sectional variance*). It is less certain that the concept also varies across times for a given unit (*process variance*). Many communication behaviors vary cross-sectionally but not over time for a given individual. For instance, while there is a lot of cross-sectional variation in habits of newspaper reading (or non-reading), only a small percentage of people change over even an extended period of time (Chaffee & Choe, 1981). Social attitudes are often defined as *enduring predispositions*, meaning we should not expect to find much process variance; the popular persuasion research concept of *attitude change* would by that definition of attitude be self-contradictory.

Time-related concepts are more difficult to specify when a researcher's unit of study is a social entity—a society, an electorate, a student body, an organization, a family, and so on. When such units are studied by sampling their membership, which is a common survey research method, change can occur for many reasons. The composition of the unit can change (old members leave or die, new ones are born or join); everyone in the unit can change at a constant rate; some members can change while others do not; or different individuals can change in different ways or at different rates. The development of methods to distinguish among these many possible processes is highly complex (see for example, Monge, 1990; Rogosa, Brandt, & Zimowski, 1982). Before adopting a particular statistical model, it is essential for the researcher to specify how he/she thinks his/her concept varies.

Cross-sectional variance among persons is often called *individual differences*, and is the subject of much research on personality and the cultural factors that help account for such differences.

Social entities can also vary cross-sectionally, but only if more than one unit is being studied; otherwise, there is no variance. Many theories closely identify communication with change and therefore with process variance. Unfortunately much exploratory work is limited to cross-sectional survey research, which is incapable of distinguishing between the results of change versus stable differences between individual units.

Conceptualizing the type of variance to expect should occur early in the process of empirical research. If, as may happen, a researcher expects change over time within individuals, but the study shows that the concept is extremely stable for the same people over a long period, it needs to be reconceptualized as a cross-sectional variable. This may in turn lead to designing a different program of research from the one originally planned. This was the experience of Ritchie, Price and Roberts (1987) in a longitudinal study of the impact of television on schoolchildren's reading skills. After a 3-year examination they found reading skill differences so stable—meaning that everyone was improving at about the same rate—that they recommended an entirely different approach to research from the one they had been pursuing.

3. Literature Search

Once we have formalized our ideas of the concept at a preliminary level, we can begin organizing the scholarly literature that deals with it. We need to find studies that either (a) involve the term we are using, even if its meaning is not the same as ours, or (b) involve the concept we are using, even if its name is not the same as our concept's. It is not necessary—nor often possible—to track down every existing study. But the literature search will be more productive if it ranges widely, finding examples of the full variety of meanings of our concept that are in use. Here, then, are some useful questions to ask while examining the literature that is found:

— What are the different conceptual meanings that have been assigned to this term, and what (if any) are their research purposes? What confusions do these ambiguities cause?

— What are the different operational definitions that have been used? Which research purposes do they serve? Which of these are related to our purposes?

— What are the usual names for these operational definitions? Are different names needed to make differences in meaning clear?

— What, considering its intended research purpose, seem to be the most promising definitions of the concept?

Operational Contingencies

Each study found in the literature has been conducted under specific conditions, such as details of time, place, and persons involved. These are contingent conditions for doing the study at all, and for the findings reported in it. Such operational contingencies, while not part of the concept per se, constrain the operational definition of each concept in a study.

Our concept will, as a rule, be intended to apply more broadly than its meaning in any specific context. For example, if we are interested in some effect of viewing television, we will find very different operational measures—in studies of children versus studies of adults, and in studies conducted during the 1950s versus those during the 1980s. Sorting out results according to these operational contingencies is one useful step in comprehending the literature. Often it can help in adjudicating conflicting findings we might encounter.

Hovland (1959) noted that controlled communication experiments often produce rather strong attitudinal effects, whereas field survey studies suggest only minimal influence. One major difference between these groups of studies is that experiments are mostly performed on students, who are much less involved in the topics under study than are the adults who are usually interviewed in surveys. Hovland suggested that adults resist media influence more than do students, which would make mass communication seem more powerful in experiments, overall, than in surveys. The operational contingency of units (students versus adults) helps to explain the differences between the experimental and survey literatures.

As operational contingencies change historically, a whole program of study may shift. An example in our time has been the concept of selective exposure to mass communication. Studies on political effects of media began in the 1940s (Berelson, Lazarsfeld, & McPhee, 1954; Lazarsfeld, Berelson, & Gaudet, 1944), when newspapers were the dominant news medium and television was in its infancy. Scholars of that time (see Klapper, 1960) concluded that "selective exposure" to media—meaning highly partisan newspapers—restricted communication impact because people were mostly reading what they already believed. In recent decades television has become the dominant medium of politics, perhaps partly because it makes selective exposure less possible. Televised partisan commercials reach a TV viewer at unpredictable times. So does news that might favor one party or candidate. When candidates debate on TV, voters are exposed about equally to the one they support, and to the opponent (Katz & Feldman, 1962). Meanwhile, major newspapers have become less partisan. Selective exposure to congenial political messages is not a ready option today, and the concept has receded to a minor position in the literature on media impact (Chaffee & Miyo, 1983). Where the operational conditions that enable an audience to select congenial messages continue, such as in specialized magazines or religious broadcasting, the behavior persists. But its relevance to the larger mass audience is diminished, and consequently so is its centrality in research conceptualization.

Operational contingencies vary across studies, but not within a given study. Indeed, within a study its contingencies of time, place, and persons are often taken for granted, given little note because they are not variable for that author. The identification of operational contingencies related to different meanings of a concept is, then, a product of the literature review. But a researcher must organize that literature in these terms. To paraphrase many studies one by one, or even to organize their titles by keywords, will not help in identifying operational contingencies that may divide the literature.

Operational contingencies are not the same as operational definitions. The operational definition of a concept is part of its explication and is selected from among a number of potential operational definitions of that concept. Operational contingencies are not concept-specific, although they can affect results that get interpreted in relation to a researcher's concept. Operational contingencies might be thought of as part of the empirical view, but not of the conceptual vision, whereas operational definitions are both.

Often the researcher has little or no practical choice of operational contingencies. Lazarsfeld, for example, decided to study the 1940 election simply because that was the time he found himself in, and he wanted to examine the role of media in an election campaign. Having limited resources, he chose one county; in 1948 he replicated the study in a second county (Chaffee & Hochheimer, 1985). Similarly, a persuasion effects experiment may be conducted on college students because they are conveniently available to the investigator, not because they are the most varied or representative target audience. Only after studies have accumulated over some years, in various locales and with different kinds of people and communication media involved, can a literature review make evident what differences these contingencies have made in the meaning of the concepts at stake.

Analysis and Synthesis

The literature review is often a study in itself. Some of the most useful advances in communication research have been analytic literature reviews. A prominent example is Rogers's *Diffusion of Innovations* (1964, 1983). By organizing and synthesizing several thousand studies of diffusion around a set of conceptual distinctions and empirical generalizations, Rogers founded an entire sub-discipline within communication research.

Another kind of literature review, and one that can be equally ground-breaking, is the critical analysis of an accumulated body of studies. Sears and Freedman (1967) reviewed several experiments that tested motivational theories of self-selection to messages that match people's pre-existing opinions. The authors explicated selective exposure by dividing the literature between studies of "voluntary exposure" and those of "de facto exposure." Their analysis of the evidence led them to conclude that the concept of voluntary selective exposure was a myth. They also concluded that people do tend to be exposed de facto to messages they agree with, but not because they particularly seek those messages for that reason. Separate studies suggest that the concept of deliberate avoidance to protect oneself from uncongenial messages is likewise a myth (Carter, Pyszka, & Guerrero, 1969). It appears that the mass communication industry is responsible for providing people with messages they approve of, without their actively doing much to affect that de facto pattern.

A literature review extends well beyond explication per se. Practically everything that follows in this outline, particularly empirical description (see Chapter 9), presumes that a literature is constantly in process. In practice the scholar begins reading prior studies, moves to various steps in the explication process, refines the preliminary definition, and then returns to the literature search with a sharpened definition. To read first the entire body of work generally related to a topic is usually much too time-consuming to be practical. One important purpose of explication is to delimit the work that needs to be done, by focusing on those studies that are relevant to the concept being formulated—and only those.

4. Processing the Literature

The literature review should yield several kinds of ideas and evidence. Primarily, it provides a picture of the variety of conceptual and operational definitions the concept has been given. These will be dealt with later in connection with meaning analysis and the design of actual research procedures. But the literature also provides descriptive information regarding the researcher's concept. This can be useful throughout conceptualization, guiding the imagination in formulating ideas, and providing expectations of what will be found in a later study.

Keep track of empirical findings while analyzing various kinds of studies. Note, for example, the distribution of values the concept seems to take on in different populations. Is it common or rare, normally distributed or skewed? How does it vary over time, or is it highly stable? What are its correlates? Is it limited to certain situations or groups (e.g., elites), or to certain periods in history or societal development (e.g., times of rapid change)?

The value of keeping track of contextual information is illustrated by Martin, McNelly, and Izcaray's (1976) study of relationships between use of different mass media. They divided the studies they found into two groups based on the correlations between media. Some surveys reported high correlations among reading newspapers, watching television, attending films, and listening to radio; further, each of these measures was correlated with the person's education and income. They put into a second group those studies where correlations among use of the different media were low, and in which education and income were not particularly associated with radio, film, or TV use. Divided in this way, the first subliterature turned out to consist almost entirely of rural surveys in Latin America, whereas the low-correlation samples were all urban and were not geographically concentrated. The authors built on this background to devise a test of the theory that media use is constrained by socioeconomic status at the low end (rural populations), but that different media are somewhat interchangeable in the typical urban condition, where structural constraints on expensive and demanding forms of media use are not so stringent. This hypothesis, which was supported, in effect modified their conceptualization of media use.

Rarity of a phenomenon can be useful in evaluating a conceptual literature. Traditional treatments of mass media effects (Katz & Lazarsfeld, 1955) emphasized the idea of a two-step flow from media to opinion leaders and thence to the public at large. But news diffusion does not work this way; most people get most of their news most of the time directly from mass media (Deutschmann & Danielson, 1960). The emphasis on personal influence in mass communication theory has declined, partly on these simple empirical grounds; in some situations it is too rare to merit special theoretical attention. In less developed countries, on the other hand, the literature still points to interpersonal channels as a major locus of influence (Rogers, 1983).

The purpose of the literature review is to guide conceptualization. All three components of the literature—meanings, operational definitions, and empirical findings—should be kept ready for reference as the researcher works through the process of explication.

5. Levels of Definition

Hempel (1952) distinguishes three levels of definition in empirical science: nominal definition, meaning analysis, and empirical analysis. These are of progressively greater utility for research in the physical sciences. For communication research, however, meaning analysis is the more central kind of work; empirical definition is an important consideration, but literally to analyze a concept's full meaning in empirical terms, as a physicist might, is highly unlikely.

This outline will follow Hempel's three levels of definition. The reader should not assume, though, that all explication leads eventually to empirical analysis in the sense that a concept can eventually be reduced to a satisfactory operational definition. Definitions in communication study are much more various, and conceived differently within separate theoretical contexts, than is the case with the physical sciences. Still, there is much to be done.

Nominal Definition

Names are often assigned to objects (e.g., *The New York Times,* Stephen, or the Sears Tower) and to classes of objects (e.g., child, memo). These nominal labels are perfectly serviceable in everyday conversation, but when applied to the more abstract ideas of communication (e.g., information, understanding, reticence) they are helpful only to the extent that they are accompanied by mutually understood linkages between the label and the object. A nominal definition is an arbitrary name that lacks linking statements; meaning analysis provides that kind of specification. A nominal definition is adopted as a convention; an empirical definition makes distinctions apparent. For example, we may consider *The Wall Street Journal* a newspaper because most of us agree that it is one (nominal definition), or because it meets certain defined criteria that distinguish newspapers from other entities.

Nominal definitions can become problematic when carried beyond their original context. For example, when electronic calculating machines were first built it seemed natural enough to call them computers. Today, though, the term *computer* doesn't describe very well what these machines do for most of us most of the time. To a young student who is learning to "write on the computer," we may have to explain a bit of history (and quite a bit about the many uses of the computer) so the conventional name is understood. Industrial etymologies account for the persistence of many now-confusing concepts in communication, such as terms from printing (e.g., the press, lower case). Words that once referred to concrete entities have become abstractions whose meanings exist independent of those roots. The basic point here is that giving some object, or idea, a name is not a definition of a concept that will carry its meaning into other contexts.

Meaning Analysis

The process of analyzing the meaning of a concept may be approached in two ways: by distillation and by list. In either case, it is useful to organize our thinking into lower-order and higher-order concepts. Lower-order concepts are closer to the world of observation, either in everyday life or in a contrived laboratory setting. A higher-order concept subsumes several lower-order concepts, and the hierarchical organization of this structure of meaning can be imagined as a definitional "tree." The trunk of this tree is the singular concept we are explicating; branching immediately from it are a few higher-order concepts; each of these can branch further into several lower-order concepts; each of these may sprout one or more operational definitions. Meaning analysis is largely an intellectual process, occupying the trunk and major branches of this structure—without totally losing sight of operationalization.

Distillation of the abstract meaning of a concept begins with reading what many different investigators have said about it.

This is followed by an intellectual process of boiling the idea down to its essential elements. What, at heart, do various writers mean by the term? The goal might be to find the central meaning of the concept, but this is rarely achieved in practice because few concepts have a single meaning that is agreed upon by all scholars. Instead, the typical product of this kind of analysis is several meanings, each of which is used by some writers.

An example of distillation is provided by Carter's (1962) identification of three different meanings of the concept of *stereotyping*. He noted that different writers used this term to refer to the polarization, fixedness, or homogenization of attitudes. In his study of an election campaign's effects, he found that only homogenization increased in relation to mass communication.

Many two-word concepts carry two (or more) meanings, but that is not always obvious in discursive writings. An example is *social reality*. McLeod and Chaffee (1972) distilled dozens of writings in which the term *social reality* was employed, usually without explicit definition. They found two quite different, in some respects opposite, meanings in this literature, which they called social REALITY (sR) and SOCIAL reality (Sr). The first (sR) gives the concept the status of an objective reality, referring to "the real social situation," a true state of affairs the writer assumes to exist even though the people in that situation might not see it. This usage of social reality is akin to the Marxist concept of *false consciousness*, in which the individual is unaware of his true, oppressed status in a stratified society. The other meaning (Sr) emphasizes instead the *un*reality of the world as it is socially defined (Berger & Luckmann, 1972). When people agree that something is so, even though it is not, they behave as if it were, and so the socially agreed-upon version of reality becomes real in its implications for people's actions. Communication is central to both concepts, sR and Sr, and they are probably best understood as intertwined with one another even though they carry different meanings. This is often the case with two-word concepts; the ambiguity becomes part of the larger concept, as in the terms *public opinion* and *mass media*. Unpacking these multiple meanings is essential if one's research is to do justice to a complex idea.

Different meanings for the same term usually come from different literatures. This is fairly common in communication, which is not always a coherent body of knowledge. Sometimes communication research is a gathering place (Schramm, 1963), a locus of overlap for several social and behavioral sciences, and for writers in literary and polemic traditions as well.

Dependency is an example of a term that means several different things within the literature of communication. Sociologists Ball-Rokeach and DeFleur (1976) use dependency to refer to a general view of mass media effects, which they suggest will be maximal on topics for which the person has no other communication source; the audience depends on the mass media. Other media researchers measure television dependency, the extent to which people who do not read print media are dependent upon television specifically for their information (e.g., McLeod & McDonald, 1985). At a more macroscopic level, Third World critical scholars see imbalanced international communication flows as part of a pattern of dependency of the less-developed nations on the Western powers (Elguea, 1984). These three distinct usages of the word *dependency* are not used in the same study, but they can easily show up on different pages of the same journal. Literature reviews in communication need to attend to meanings, not just terminology.

Definition by list consists of identifying all the lower-order concepts that constitute your higher-order concept. The definitional tree is an organized list; the Linnaean classification system in biology is a prominent example.

The concept of mass media is usually defined by list rather than by distillation of its core meaning, which is ambiguous. (Does *mass* refer to mass production, or to a conception of the audience as a mass, or to both?) Grammatically, *media* is a plural noun (the singular is *medium*), and the basic list is fairly well known. It includes newspapers and books and magazines, television, radio, and films. Most of the time such a list suffices, and it can be broken down into a tree form, such as division between print and audio-visual media; or within, say, television, division into broadcast, video, and cable. An economist trying to estimate the contribution the mass media make to Gross National Product (e.g., Machlup, 1962) might spend some time creating a more satisfying list, but a simple one would meet most scholarly needs.

A crisis can occur in a definitional list when a new item appears that might belong on it. A distillation of meaning may be demanded, where an agreed-upon list had sufficed before. At one time, for example, there was no need for the term *mass media*. The concept of printing sufficed until about a century ago; *mass media* was created as a concept to accommodate twentieth-century innovations. Is it still useful in our era of new communication technologies? Cable television and video rentals seem easily added to the mass media list. But inclusion of interactive systems (e.g., videotext, videodisc) would depend a lot on one's definition, which in turn depends on its purpose. Electronic mail, for example, would not belong on most lists, but for some purposes it might be included. If it is, a new distillation—and perhaps a term other than *mass media*—will be needed. A list is mainly a convenience to the user, but scholars are interdependent and their conceptual decisions can affect one another.

A list does not simply expand over time. Old forms may die out and vanish from the list. For instance, such mass communication forms as the *broadside* and the *newsreel*, which today's list-makers might ponder where to put, no longer exist in sufficient prominence to be worth the trouble. A list, although an imperfect method of concept explication, is often productive enough. It is not necessary to think in an organized way about all the forms a concept might take, just to study one or a few of them. In other words, when a list will do, let it do.

Definition by list might appear at first blush to be easier to achieve than the more abstract distillation, with its demanding program of reading and analysis of disparate statements about a concept. But the two procedures are not distinct. In the process of organizing a list, such as a definitional tree, one begins to formulate at least an implicit set of empirical rules.

Definition by list alone, even if it is a very thoughtful and defensible list, is isolated between two important limitations. Behind it lies the problem of explaining what rules have been followed in building the list. In effect, to make a list we must have some implicit attribute(s), which is to say a theoretical analysis. Thus a list that is built *after* an explication is much more useful than a list that is simply cooked up for the immediate occasion of providing examples or grouping them.

A second limitation of a list is that it is time-bound, always subject to change. Any given list is limited to the reality of what exists at the moment. In the absence of further definition, there is no way of knowing whether an innovation should (or could) be added to the list. For instance, the concept of *network evening news* in the United States was for some years represented by a list of three broadcast networks: NBC, CBS, and ABC, each with a national news program at approximately the dinner hour. Then Cable News Network was formed, transmitting news around the clock. One question for the scholar is whether *evening* has been merely a convenient part of the name (i.e., a nominal definition) or if presentation of news in the early evening is of particular interest. The list alone does not tell you why it includes what it does.

Nor does a list inspire the imagination. Inventions, such as an around-the-clock news channel, are evoked by conceptualization—not by a mere listing of what already exists. Likewise in research, a new concept can open the path to discovery.

A *typology* is an organized list based on two or more attributes, hierarchically ordered. A rule is used to apply an attribute to the task of classification, so a typology can be thought of as a list based on several rules. A list based on only one rule, then, consists of the representations of a single attribute, and can be thought of as an index. In some studies *mass media use,* for example, is represented by a single index; while in others, it is analyzed as a typology built on several attributes.

Empirical Definition

Hempel (1952) considered empirical analysis of a concept the ultimate goal of explication in the physical sciences. He envisioned the formation of concepts that, through empirical research, would eventually be specified in operational terms. The concept of *hardness,* for example, was operationalized by the scratch test: If one material can cut a scratch in another, it is harder—both by definition and in fact.

No such hard-and-fast definitions are at hand in the study of human communication, nor are they likely to be. Despite considerable enthusiasm for "communication science" (Berger & Chaffee, 1987), attempts to reduce any concept in communication to a set of empirical referents have met with frustration. Human beings are too various, in their behaviors and their meanings, for us to arrive at a single fully satisfactory operationalization of any important concept.

We do, however, have empirical definitions of a more modest kind. An empirical definition of a concept enables us to conclude whether an event we encounter is an instance of that concept or not. This means that the definition tells us what to look for to make decisions about both inclusion and exclusion. Empirical rules specify conditions that researchers require so that when they discuss their research, their evidence coincides with their meaning. The empirical referents are part of the concept, but not identical with it. Just as an instance is only part of a concept (and vice versa), empirical research is only part of a body of conceptual discourse (and vice versa). As Blalock (1968) puts it, we have *auxiliary theories* linking our concepts with our measures; these measurement theories are tested as part of the test of a substantive theory that includes them. Research may also be designed to test the measurement theory itself.

Empirical definition is a goal toward which explication works. The assumption is that the more clearly researchers can specify what their concept means in the world of human experience, the more they know about it and the more knowledge they can contribute to others. This assumption has proven itself worthwhile in a thousand and more programs of communication research.

An example of research working toward an empirical definition is found in Festinger's studies on the psychological concept of *cognitive dissonance*. He originally defined dissonance quite broadly, as a noxious state that can be aroused in a person who holds two cognitions "one of which implies the obverse of the other" (Festinger, 1957). Dissonance theory became for a time highly productive, generating many experimental tests related to communication (Brehm & Cohen, 1962); but in experimental situations where the subjects had not yet acted, researchers often failed to find hypothesized effects. Festinger, not wanting to abandon an idea that had served well, decided that a demarcation was needed between dissonance and a related concept, *cognitive conflict*. So he proposed *decision* (or public commitment to a decision) as his new boundary (Festinger, 1964). Up to the point of decision, the person can experience conflict; only after a decision is made would the same person experience dissonance. Although it cut back Festinger's concept of cognitive dissonance from the broader sweep it had once seemed to offer, this boundary preserved it. Dissonance theory came to be viewed as applicable to a narrower range of behavior than originally envisioned, but within this reduced domain the concept remained viable. The point here is that the rule concerning decision was an empirical one.

Rules that can be applied to many phenomena have a number of advantages. They do not change historically the way lists do. They can even be applied "in theory" to events that have never occurred, providing a guide to experimental creation of unique conditions. But empirical rules are not easy to come by. They grow out of a sustained program of research, so early on they are heavily dependent upon meaning analysis. When first conceived, a rule is tested as a hypothesis, and only if it passes its test is it likely to become a definitional proposition that other scholars will adopt.

Required observations. How does a researcher decide when to infer that the concept exists? An empirical definition specifies the observations that are required. This involves several steps already covered here, such as unit definition, specification of attributes, and time points or other comparisons that must be made.

Just as units of observation may be either individual or relational (e.g., "husbands" are defined only in relation to wives), attributes may be conceived as either properties or relationships. Most variables in communication are measured in a relative fashion; to say that a person is "intelligent," or "conservative," for example, usually describes that individual's location in a distribution for a large population. What is less obvious, and more critical conceptually, is that many communication attributes are relationship *concepts,* not just relational measures. For example, to be "persuasive" a person must persuade someone else; to be a "conformist" one must conform to some social norm; in these cases, either the other person or the general norm is part of the concept, not just the operational definition. In specifying required observations, these components of the meaning need to be retained in the empirical definition.

One way of phrasing the problem of empirical definition is in terms of the criteria that must be met before we would infer that the concept exists in a particular case. These include criteria of both necessity and sufficiency, which are related to the terms *necessary and sufficient conditions* in causal inference.

A necessity is a criterion that must be met, or else the existence of the concept is impossible. Showing empirically that something is necessary is no simple matter, and attributes that are literally necessary are rare in communication study. More often, we set sufficiency as our criterion, in that any of several observations might satisfy our meaning of the concept. Sufficiency implies that the concept in question *does* occur if the criterion is met, which is often what is tested in empirical research.

There may be a number of different conditions under which the concept is instantiated, and each may be sufficient. No one of them is necessary. For example, viewing Channel 2 news is sufficient as an instance of the concept "viewing of TV news" but it is not a necessity; observing that a person instead views news on Channel 5 or Channel 7 would satisfy the concept just as well. This is an example of the kind of empirical definition that emerges from a meaning analysis that consists of a list of lower-order concepts.

Analysis by distillation generally leads toward higher-order concepts. Sometimes the concept is overly abstract and cannot be satisfactorily explicated in terms of required observations. For example, we might define the concept *relational communication* as requiring two persons (A and B), and a relationship (AB) between them. Relational communication occurs when A acts in a way that B interprets as signaling what A's perception of the AB relationship is. Many conceptual decisions need to be made about the observation of A and B. Must A have a perception of the AB relationship? Must A's signal match it? Must B's interpretation of it match as well? Must this affect B's perception of the AB relationship? If so, must B's perception change in a direction closer to A's? Only if most of these questions are answered positively could we define relational communication as a process of convergence of perceptions in an AB relationship. But if we do answer them positively, and if we take literally the idea of empirical definition, we would be faced with many, probably too many, observations to make. An empirical definition should not place an impossible burden on the empirical investigator.

Some researchers use only part of a full concept to identify their required observations. For example, one might be satisfied to infer that relational communication has occurred if A and B converge over time in their perceptions of the AB relationship.

When this convergence does not occur, though, the researcher is left to wonder which elements were missing—and which were necessary to the concept in the first place. A different researcher might instead be satisfied with observation of overt messages about the AB relationship (e.g., "I like you," "We're really communicating," or, "Leave me alone"). A third might want to include nonverbal cues (e.g., dress, body position, eye contact). Each researcher is changing the definition in substantial ways by deciding what is to be observed, and each specific definition drives a particular study. The closer a researcher's empirical definition gets to operational definition, which is to say the more that a higher-order term is replaced with a lower-order term, the narrower his/her concept becomes. At this point in this example, each researcher should sense that the starting concept of *relational communication* is too broad, and some qualifying terminology is needed so that the different usages in these projects are not confused.

Formal operations. The term *formal* refers here to formulas for mathematical operations that are performed on empirical data. These procedures are part of the operational definition of a concept, so they should be carefully designed to conform to the conceptual definition. Formal procedures include at least three steps: measurement, scaling, and statistics.

At each step, it is important to keep in mind the concept that is under study. Formal operations are themselves mindless; they are purely formulaic and can have no idea what the researcher is trying to accomplish. Measures, scales, and statistical procedures are tools, but they do not in themselves represent concepts. The researcher is responsible for selecting those tools that suit the task at hand.

Measurement consists of the assignment of symbols, typically numbers, to observations. Numbers are much easier to work with than are the observations themselves. Even purely qualitative, unordered attributes are assigned categorical numbers (e.g., 0 = male, 1 = female) so that they can easily be converted to percentages, or added to other qualitative categories to create quantitative indices. The advent of computers has strengthened the clerical tendency to replace qualitative meanings with numbers; it is all too easy to lose track of these meanings when one is scanning computer output.

In replacing a set of observations with a set of numbers, be sure to retain all the information that the concept requires. The explication should specify what this includes; if it does not, it needs more work. Spending time "up front" on explication can help avoid losing key information because the researcher failed to anticipate the need for it.

Coding of communication content is a popular measurement activity that is common to the study of interpersonal interactions, mass media messages, and open-ended responses in survey interviews, for example. Explication should be an ongoing process throughout; preliminary classification rules become refined as a researcher progresses through practice coding. Much communication content is available in precoded form, but other people's codes have been designed for their purposes and will rarely fit someone else's. Reeves (1989) notes that, for example, traditional categories of television programs (e.g., news, entertainment, advertising) do not necessarily correspond to the variables that affect psychological processing.

A single set of messages can be classified in many ways, and the few categories chosen need to be defined carefully. The three general principles for coding are as follows:

a. There should be a place for everything; this is often called the principle of *collectively exhaustive* categories.
b. There should be only one category for each unit; this is the principle of *mutually exclusive* categories.
c. Each set of categories should be defined according to a single classificatory rule.

The first two principles are addressed by preliminary formulation of categories, partly through trial and error. Coding is to some extent inductive; if a type of item occurs with unanticipated frequency, it may even lead to a new focal variable. Reformulation proceeds until coders largely agree on the classification of items. The third principle is the most intellectual task in content coding. It does not mean that only one attribute can be used; but it does mean that each attribute used to form a typology should be separately explicated.

A coding scheme requires explication not only of the rules for classification (i.e., the dimension along which items vary) but also of the boundaries between categories. For example, Butler and Paisley (1980) created a feminist "Consciousness" scale for coding sexism in the mass media. Their lowest level is called "Put her down"; the highest is "Recognize that she is non-stereotypic"; in between are other categories: "Keep her in her place," "Give her two places," and "Acknowledge that she is equal." These categories are treated as mutually exclusive, arrayed in an ordinal scale; the boundaries are substantively significant, not merely convenient.

Scaling evolves from measurement when decisions are made about the numbers to assign to observations. In the classic typology of scales (Stevens, 1946), every scale is at least nominal, which is to say any measure gives a unique name (or number) to each category into which units are classified. Successively higher forms of order are possible: ordinal scales, equal-interval scales, and ratio scales. The choice should be based on explication, particularly a simultaneous consideration of the latent continuum and the operational scale.

In explication consider first whether to treat the concept as either a continuous or a discrete variable. A continuous variable has an infinite series of values; personal intelligence is an example. A discrete variable is a set of categories that are inherently discontinuous; one cannot shade into the other. Two common discrete variables in everyday life are pregnancy and death. We even have little jokes (an acceptable adjunct to explication, if apt) to describe the discreteness; one cannot be "a little bit pregnant" or "slightly dead."

Although we think of some concepts as continuous variables, none of our operational scales can be. Measures consist entirely of discrete categories, even though some analog devices come close to continuous measurement. We conventionally break down distance, for example, into arbitrary categories, such as inches, miles, or light-years. These are discrete categories; if the latent variable is continuous, some instances will be classified together that are technically different.

Refining categories for exact classification can be a costly effort, and there is no point in being more precise than the research problem requires. The span represented by a scale interval should be fine enough to detect differences the researcher expects to be meaningful in the phenomena being studied. Reeves, Thorson, and

Schleuder (1986) considered this issue in the measurement of time concepts in communication.

An ordinal scale may be created from observations of either continuous or discrete phenomena, as long as each succeeding level can be conceived as "greater than" the last. Most scales in communication research are ordinal, which makes them compatible with theoretical statements of the popular form, "The greater variable X, then the greater variable Y."

Dichotomous (but ordinal) categories can be combined to create a more extensive ordinal scale. For example, the two dichotomies "pregnant-nonpregnant" and "alive-dead" could be combined to track the history of one man from before the time his mother became pregnant (0), to when he was a fetus (1), to the "lifetime" between his birth and his death (2), to the time after he died (3). These categories are ordinal, but the intervals are clearly not equal; indeed, the two extreme categories (0 and 3) have no outer boundaries.

Equal-interval scaling consists of assigning numbers such as 0-1-2-3-4-5 and then treating them in statistical analysis as if the distances between adjacent numbers were equal. That is, it is assumed that $5-4 = 4-3 = 3-2 = 2-1 = 1-0$. When the underlying variable is a continuum (e.g., time) this is usually appropriate. But those conditions are not often met, and treating an ordinal scale as an equal-interval scale often creates error.

An equal-interval scale may also be a ratio scale, which means that it has a true zero point. Only when intervals are equal, and where zero really means the total absence of the condition, can one perform the full range of mathematical operations. Formally, a ratio scale is so called because ratios that appear algebraically equal are in fact equal. That is, for example, $1/2 = 2/4 = 3/6 = 40/80$, and so on. Mathematically, a ratio constitutes division; this is another way of saying that any formal operation that involves division requires a ratio scale.

Ratio scales are often hard to justify in communication research because they assume a zero point as well as equal-interval properties. For many of our concepts the variation is from "more" to "less" but the notion of "zero" would be hard to define.

Rescaling, or transformation of a scale by a mathematical formula, is one method of correcting for the common problem of a ratio scale whose numerical intervals do not correspond to its conceptual intervals. Logarithmic transformations are often used for this purpose. The log of income, for instance, is a better representation of functional differences between strata than is income expressed in raw dollars. It can be ludicrous to equate the difference between two people who make $10,000 and $20,000, respectively, with the difference between two who make $510,000 and $520,000. But if we convert the dollar scale to a positive logarithm, the latter difference becomes properly trivial. Conclusions based on logarithmic (or other) transformations should be couched in appropriate terms; the analyses involved are not valid for the original (raw data) scale.

One of the earliest attitudinal scaling methods started with paired comparisons (dichotomous ordinal data) and combined them to yield an equal-interval attitude scale (Thurstone & Chave, 1929). For a description of this method, consult Edwards (1957). Multidimensional scaling, which is extensively used in the measurement of communication variables today, also begins with paired comparisons data.

Sometimes the research purpose calls for breaking down a single ordinal continuum into two variables. Newspaper reading habits provide an example. Some people never read a newspaper (many because they cannot), while others read one or more every day; still others read occasionally or often, which are intermediate categories. This is certainly an ordinal continuum, but depending on what we want to study, it may represent two concepts: reading (dichotomous), and amount of reading (continuous). If the purpose is to analyze differences between nonreaders and readers, the higher categories on the full scale might well be merged into one (all "readers," regardless of frequency). If, on the other hand, the search is for explanations of the amount of reading, it might be advisable to eliminate people who never read a newspaper from your study entirely.

Statistical analysis begins with descriptive statistics such as those of central tendency and dispersion of the variable's distribution. What is to be described depends not only on the measure itself, but also on its conceptual definition. Bivariate analyses too should be anticipated conceptually, and selection of a statistical model is governed partly by the kind of scale created. Use of statistical analyses in evaluating an operational definition is discussed in Chapter 9.

Formal operations, such as measurement, scaling, and statistical techniques, do not constitute definitions of concepts in themselves. It is safe to assume that no statistical formula was ever created with a concept of human communication in mind. Explication puts the researcher in the position of determining conceptually what formal procedures are appropriate for the concept, rather than attempting to find meanings that might express the results of a particular formula.

6. Review of Definition

The steps covered to this point produce a preliminary definition of the researcher's concept, from meaning to observation to formal operations. This is a start, but not in itself an explication. It is now time to apply vocabulary criteria to our preliminary definition. After reviewing the principles and queries in this section, it is quite likely that we will decide to revise the definition.

Specificity

One straightforward criterion for evaluating the preliminary definition is the degree of specificity it embodies. In general, be specific. For example, operational definitions of "television viewing" are more specific than those of "media use," and time spent in public affairs discussion "yesterday" is a more specific measure than "daily." One good reason for specificity is that researchers can always combine data from several specific measures to create an estimate of a more general concept, but the reverse is not true. An operational definition that tried to cover too much under one indicator cannot be broken down into its constituent parts after the fact. For example, if we measure "media use" and do not get the result we expect from it, there is no way to ascertain where the fault lies—in our conceptual definition, or our operational definition of it. It may be that the hypothesis tested was

accurate for, say, "newspaper use" but not for "TV use"; only if
we have a more specific measure for each can we check out this
possibility. If this suspicion turns out to be correct, it should lead
to explication of these more specific concepts.

Reification

To reify is to treat an abstract concept as a thing. We often use
terms, such as *group mind, momentum,* or *mental set,* to represent
conditions that may not exist except in our imagination. It is easy
to reify with words, which once spoken make it seem as though
the term has existential import. Explication should alert us to
this kind of verbal trap.

Communication itself is a potential reification, and so are
many of the terms related to it. The essential question to be
asked here is whether we have evidence—other than our own belief—that the concept has empirical referents.

A surprising number of terms used in everyday discourse about
communication may not pass this simple test. One of the most common terms in the history of persuasion research, for example, is
attitude. No one has ever seen an attitude, although our belief in its
existence may be strong. Methods to measure attitudes are among
the earliest empirical traditions (e.g., Thurstone & Chave, 1929). Extensive explications have been devoted to this concept (e.g., Edwards, 1957; Green, 1954). But unless we assume that either a
widespread belief in a concept or a technique of measurement is evidence of existence, then the concept of attitude remains on shaky
ground.

To call into question the existence of a concept is not to say it
does not exist, but simply to make that an empirical question. In
public opinion research, for example, there is a natural skepti-
cism about the opinions people express in polls: Did they have
opinions before they were asked? When operational definitions,
such as question wording or sequence, differ from one survey to
the next, there is a pragmatic approach to the reification issue. If
the distribution of pros and cons on a public question is about
the same even when the question is asked in very different ways,
these opinions are probably real enough. Opinions on abortion
of a fetus with birth defects are not much affected by question

order, but asking this item influences later responses regarding abortion if the woman "does not want any more children" (Bishop, Oldendick, & Tuchfarber, 1985; Schuman, Presser, & Ludwig, 1981). On the latter issue, a lot of people seem not to hold a settled opinion. If the proportion endorsing an opinion statement shifts dramatically with only minor variations in question order or wording, the data may represent little regarding public sentiment (Payne, 1951).

A sound approach to reification is to attempt to establish the existence of the attribute in question before conducting research that assumes it. Consider Iyengar's (1987) work on people's interpretations of causality in TV news about societal problems. He began by asking people simply to describe their thoughts about such news topics as poverty and unemployment. More than half the time, respondents said they thought of these as problems and they also thought about what causes those problems. With the existence of such causal thoughts established, Iyengar then went on to experiment on the effects of different versions of newscasts on these causal perceptions.

Invariance of Usage

We do not use every word to mean the same thing every time; our language is much too rich, and our lives much too varied, for that. One long-run goal of concept explication is to establish a scientific meaning for each term. It follows, then, that we should use that term consistently to refer to that concept, and not to conflate it with related concepts or alternative usages of the term. If we are not consistent in our application of scientific language, it is unlikely that anyone else will be. The converse does not hold, of course; being consistent ourselves is merely a small step, not one that guarantees emulation unless we demonstrate to others in our discipline that our usage pays intellectual dividends.

The criterion of invariance would be trivial if applied only to ourselves. It is also a test to apply to others: Which writers use the concept consistently? Intellectual work is fragmented into schools of thought, and we can examine the literature to see which usages are common—and consistent—within various traditions. Some groups of scholars are more cohesive than others in matters of definition.

If a term is used casually to mean different things by people who cite one another frequently, there may be a need for continued explication. In mass communication the term *knowledge gap* refers to a process of widening social differences as a result of an information campaign (Tichenor, Donohue, & Olien, 1970). Perhaps because the term itself sounds like a static condition, however, it sometimes gets diminished to mean little more than a predictable difference in information levels between social strata. The powerful conception of the knowledge gap as a process, and as an inadvertent societal dysfunction that a campaign might be designed to avoid (Rogers, 1976), gets lost. To some extent this is due to a purposeful ambiguity in the term, but variance in usage is a risk of ambiguous terminology.

Some writers delight in using an ambiguous term to point up a number of thoughts at one time. There is nothing wrong with this practice—and it often makes for delightful reading—but it should not be confused with explication of a concept. It is an exercise in the variousness of meanings, but not an attempt to focus upon a useful one for further study.

In qualitative studies of communication—itself something of a misnomer since all communication research relies upon qualitatively defined concepts—Christians and Carey (1981) argue for the utility of "sensitized concepts" (see also Blumer, 1954) rather than explication. A loosely defined idea has the value of sensitizing the researcher to many possible instances of it. This approach calls for a different kind of specification, leaves open the issue of reification, and intentionally makes room for considerable variance in usage. Christians and Carey give examples of provocative phrases, such as Veblen's concept of *conspicuous consumption,* which suggest certain kinds of phenomena but do not narrowly define what to observe. An extreme form of ambiguity is the oxymoron, a compound term whose parts seem inherently at odds with one another. Riesman's *lonely crowd* is a good example. The point Christians and Carey are making is that one should not attempt to define these terms with great specificity, lest they be stripped of their sensitizing capacity. This approach is independent of explication. A sensitizing concept is speculative, a way of "seeing with new eyes," and could well be a tool in an early stage of scientific investigation.

Invariance of usage, then, is relative in some degree to the stage to which a program of research has progressed. In early stages there is likely to be a good deal of ambiguity and flexible usage, as part of an open-minded orientation to phenomena to be studied. Theories about communication come not only from participation and observation, but also from thinking about those experiences. If, however, variance within the same writer or the same intellectual tradition does not at some point begin to shrink so that meanings become focused, we should suspect that rather little progress is being made toward understanding.

No concept in communication research is likely to refer to identical operations and meanings across the full range of investigators, theorists, writers, and users of knowledge. A kind of discipline can be said to exist, though, when there is a group of scientists who use a set of terms consistently—even if most people do not. In physics, for instance, the terms *energy* and *work* have quite explicit meanings; they are definable in terms of simple formulas, which every physicist understands within a clearly bounded theoretical system. Those who have not studied physics often do not understand these meanings and may use these same words in many other ways. The word *mass* in mass communication, for example, has rather little to do with its meaning in physics.

Invariance of usage of a term across a large number of scholars and scientists cannot be accomplished by fiat, despite the hopes of some dictionary writers in circumscribed disciplines. In the long run consistency grows out of need when a large number of studies point in the same direction. Scientists have to communicate their research to one another without extensive face-to-face conversation. Concept explication, from the specification of criteria to the standardization of formal operations, helps a great deal toward this end. If we find scholars using the same term to mean quite different things, or using different words to refer to the same concept, we can conclude that the explication process has yet to be achieved at the level of the discipline as a whole.

7. Modified Definition

Having evaluated our definition according to the criteria in Chapter 6, we may wish to rethink our explication. Often a scholar gets to this point and decides to start over, recognizing the pitfalls of what seemed at the start like a good idea.

The next step in explication is to set forth boundaries for the concept; the observations that need to be made to instantiate it; and the formal operations that are to be performed on these observations. The careful scholar returns to these considerations often, working between meaning and observation to formulate a tentative, modified definition for further research.

8. Operational Procedures

Deciding what to do empirically is a critical point in any research project, and a very unsettling time if we are doing the job properly. Large decisions face us. Textbooks on research methods typically frame these as choices among major classes of methods, such as content analysis, sample survey, or laboratory experiment. But those are venues for observation, and first we need to know what we are trying to observe. That has been the purpose of our explication. The choice of method should flow from the definition we are reaching.

The operational definition should take precedence over other decisions regarding operational procedures. In principle, we seek to study people and contexts that are most appropriate to our concept, not vice versa. In practice, there is a good deal of compromise at this stage. We study communication because we are interested in the people and the contexts, and some are more interesting to us than others. But there is a difference between studying college students because our concept is particularly suited to them, and because they are easily available to us. At the least, we must take care that the real-world settings we select for study do not constrain the variation we are seeking to capture in our operational definition.

Research methods are not intended to be covered fully or systematically in this book. There are many texts on research design, data collection, statistical analysis, and other features of operational research. Here we will touch on these matters only as they bear upon concept explication. References will be limited to methods that are fairly standard within traditional communication study. The reader interested in other methods will, it is hoped, carry conceptual concerns into those domains.

Passive Versus Active Observation

A first-order question to consider is whether the observations our explication requires already occur. If not, we may have to make them occur, that is, create them. Communication is often conceived as a way of making some other condition occur; if that occurrence is not easily observable, the investigator may have to either create novel communications or impose exposure to specific, selected communications for the people in whom the condition is to occur. This procedure is common in experimental research on communication effects. The principle extends to any condition required according to the concept explication. The general question for the investigator is whether to adopt a passive observer's role, or to take an active part in creating the conditions necessary for observation.

A great deal of work in communication research consists of active observation in this extended sense. Archives, for example, are created for use in research. There are stacks of newspapers and private collections of videotapes all about. To create an archive suitable for systematic content analysis, though, is expensive, laborious, and space-consuming, an ongoing activity to which only a very few research libraries commit themselves.

Record keeping is another common form of data creation. People communicate thousands or millions of times (depending upon the explication) a day, but neither they nor others keep many records of those events. Indeed, to keep a thorough record can constrain the communication behavior so that it would be quite unrealistic as a representation of natural events. Csikszentmihalyi and Kubey (1981) have devised a method of randomly sampling people's communication behavior throughout the day by signaling them with a radio "beeper" each time the person is to fill out a brief self-report form.

Experimentation is built upon actively created data, in the form of the manipulated (independent) variable at least. Events are made to occur so the researcher can be confident of observing them. A subject can be exposed to a message that does not exist outside the experimental laboratory, and responses may be elicited that likewise could not occur anywhere else. For instance, Bandura, Ross, and Ross (1961) compared children's play behaviors after seeing a live or filmed adult "model" attack (punch, kick) an inflatable doll. Later, in a test situation, the child's toys included a similar inflatable doll; the operational issue was whether the children would imitate the model's attack. None of this hitting and kicking, filmed or otherwise, would have occurred were it not for this study, although one underlying reason for the experiment was that in real life some children do all too much hitting and kicking.

The survey researcher may rely on a respondent's ability to recall communication events after some time. Survey interviewers often aid recall with detailed question formats, supplementary diaries, and other devices that help the person succeed as a self-observing participant in the research.

Survey research is an intermediate method with respect to the passive-active observational continuum. That is, surveys often mix both kinds of data. Many interview questions would not occur to respondents who are not in the study; one-quarter of interviewees may give opinions even about fictitious matters unless they are offered a negative cue, such as, "Do you have an opinion on this or not?" (Bishop, Oldendick, Tuchfarber, & Bennett, 1980). The researcher runs the risk of mistaking created data for observed events; all that has been observed, technically at least, is that the person has been asked a certain question and has given a particular response to it on that occasion.

The existential status of actively created data needs to be considered carefully. Active methods for observation are tools, and their creation—in the form of laboratory procedures, interviewing methods, participant observation, and even speculative concepts—is a central activity of any science. Methods are designed to facilitate observation; what happens is no more nor less "real" than are events that occur "naturally" without special action on the part of the investigator. An active researcher is simply operating in a way that enables difficult observations to be made. The data result from creative effort that is directed at learning something about our world and the people in it. Such effort is as natural as other events, but bear in mind that the actions of the investigator are part of the concept's operational definition.

When we want to know what might happen if certain previously unobserved conditions obtain, we may need to create conditions that otherwise might not present themselves. Pilot tests, feasibility studies, and formative research are examples. If results are promising, such experimental research often leads to large-scale innovation. *Sesame Street*, the highly successful preschool educational television series, was laboriously pretested in many experimental formats before it was ever broadcast to the "real world" of family living rooms (Palmer, 1981).

The choice between observing naturally occurring events and created events is determined mainly by the definition of the researcher's concept, but to an extent it is also a matter of intellectual style. Some researchers prefer to maximize ties to the everyday world by limiting themselves to passive observations of events they know would occur anyway. Content analysts think of their work this way, as do those survey researchers who seek unobtrusive measures of communication behavior (Webb, Campbell, Schwartz, & Sechrest, 1966). Other investigators are more concerned with extending the range of their concepts to less commonplace occurrences that they see as theoretically significant. Some highly original experimenters fit this description, as do many communication scientists who, having explicated concepts that extend beyond the range of everyday occurrence, contrive unique observational methods to find instances of hard-to-find phenomena. The line is not clear-cut. For example, a classic study of how people use media was built around the unusual event of a newspaper strike; subscribers could then see what "missing the newspaper" meant to them (Berelson, 1949).

Each approach, emphasizing active or passive observation, has its contribution to make. Most students of communication tend to specialize in one approach but not both. The particular methods in either case require a good deal of study and experience to master. What is central to explication is that the choice be made knowingly, and that the researcher know how to operationalize a concept one way or the other.

Units of Observation

Selection of the kind of unit to observe in the field or laboratory should flow directly from the researcher's unit definition for the concept. Unfortunately this is not always the case. For example, attributes of social systems are often operationalized via individual-level data collection. Units that represent mental and social events, such as decisions, are often tied to individuals as well. Over-reliance on the individual as the locus of data collection (such as a survey respondent) is often due to convenience. It is easier to observe, say, a parent or a child than a parent-child relationship as a unit. The researcher's explication should not be forgotten upon entering the field situation and operationalizing the concept.

Sampling

If an explication limits a concept to a specific population of units, special sampling procedures may be called for. In mass communication, concepts often apply only to particular populations, such as owners of videocassette recorders (Cohen, Levy, & Golden, 1988) or the audience for daytime serials on radio (Herzog, 1944) or television (Cantor & Pingree, 1983). For such studies, simple random sampling procedures are often inappropriate, and the investigator may need to devise purposive methods such as stratified sampling.

Sometimes we encounter the other extreme—demanding a random sample of some very large population (e.g., U.S. adults) for no conceptual reason. A general population sample guarantees there will be considerable variation in the data set, and extrapolation of results to a definable population is sometimes desirable for substantive or rhetorical purposes. But unless the explication is specific to that population, this rather costly kind of sampling is not justifiable on conceptual grounds alone. Realizing this, communication researchers who are pursuing an empirically demanding concept concentrate their resources instead on theoretically relevant features of data collection.

9. Evaluation of Operational Definition

Empirical Description

The first stage in evaluating an operational definition at work is to examine the statistical properties of the data it generates. At the simplest level, is there variation? Does the number of cases in various categories seem reasonable? Is the range of values approximately what we expected? Is the variable normally distributed, or otherwise suitable for any statistical plans we might have had for it?

In pretesting an operational definition, the answers to such questions begin to accumulate rapidly. We need only one or two dozen cases to address some of these questions, so we can pick out wildly unsatisfactory measures. If our measure seems to be far from what we anticipated, we may want to adjust it immediately. This is easily done in content analysis, but equally important when measuring people.

A researcher's first experience with data tends to shift attention to the data—and away from the concept. It is essential to remember, during pretesting and adjustment of operational definitions, what concept those data are intended to represent.

Operational data may confront the researcher with ambiguous cases, units that do not fit into the categories set out a priori—or units that seem to fit into two or more categories. These problems of missing data and ambiguity need to be identified early in the empirical research process, so they will not mushroom into accumulated masses of unusable cases later. A clear rule for resolving ambiguity, or for "missing data" cases, should be integrated into the explication. In survey research, for example, people's answers to some questions may be missing because of clerical errors in the interview, but if more than, say, 5% of respondents do not answer a question, there is probably some substantive reason, and the missing cases should be handled thoughtfully. It might be wisest to ignore all missing-data cases, or to assign them all the lowest possible value on the scale, or a middling value such as the group mean or mode, or the midpoint of the response scale. Each of these choices represents a different conceptual meaning, and should be made by the researcher—not, as can easily be done, by the default option in a computer data-analysis package.

Comparison to Prior Literature

Our expectations for our measures grow partly out of prior research we have reviewed on the subject. We must not lose sight of it. Usually we should encounter quite a bit of parallel, if not identical, empirical evidence in not only our review of the literature but also our early data analyses. As we begin to accumulate our own data, we need to array it (at least mentally) alongside similar measures from previous studies. Are the pretest estimates of central tendency and distribution, for example, within the general range other studies led us to anticipate? If not, should they be?

Prior and concurrent literature help in interpreting any single operational definition. Particularly, convergent results from several different methods lend a sense of validity to each study. For example, various audience surveys regarding the 1976 presidential candidate debates asked several kinds of questions about related concepts, and got estimates in the same range (Sears & Chaffee, 1979). A national poll by the Roper agency found that 14% felt the debates had been "very informative"; another survey found that 16% considered them "very revealing"; and in a third study 21% said they had learned something new and important about issues from the debates. Those results for self-perceived learning, all in the same fairly low range, provide convergent validation for one another.

Adequacy of Operational Definition

Is our operational definition still a manifestation of the concept we intended? As we begin refining our operational definition to meet empirical expectations, it may begin to stray from the original theoretical intention. It is important to keep an eye on both concept and measure. For example, some researchers are interested in "sexuality" on television. A content analysis would rarely find explicit depictions of sexual acts; this operational definition is probably too demanding. On the other hand, if all non-work-related male-female interactions on TV get included, much of the content coded will not correspond to the concept intended.

Modified Conceptual Definition

At this point, we have undoubtedly modified our concept from what we began with, to bring it into line with operational realities. We need to return to our original meaning analysis to see what has been lost or added. Is the operationalized concept we are now working with suitable for the purposes we originally had in mind? If not, we may need to make some decisions, such as to rename the concept to match the new meaning we are giving it, or to abandon the original idea altogether.

For example, the term *information* conjures up many substantive meanings having to do with education, knowledge, news, facts, computerized data bases, empirical statistics, and the like. But in much of the communication literature the term is used in a restricted and formal sense, based on Information Theory and the mathematical concept of entropy or uncertainty (Ritchie, 1991). By equating *information* with *entropy*, a communication scientist abandons most of the other meanings of the first term. This practice bothers other scholars, who want to use *information* to refer to other conditions, and they may recommend that *entropy*, a term of more limited currency than *information*, be used when entropy is precisely what is meant. Ironically, that was the position of Shannon (1949), whose formulas became known as Information Theory, despite his insistence to the contrary.

10. Univariate Research

Once a concept is operationalized, it should be studied as a research topic in itself. For convenience, this will be called "univariate research," used in a broad manner to refer to a number of different kinds of empirical inquiry related to a concept. These include descriptive statistics, mentioned earlier, and tests of reliability and validity.

Not all concepts are variables, and some concepts consist of several variables or have many indicators. For instance, *interaction* is a non-variable concept; *frequency of interaction* is a variable. *Ritual* may not be a variable, but it includes several dimensions that may be present or absent in a given case (Rothenbuhler, 1988). The term *univariate* here is not meant to exclude those kinds of concepts. The main point of this section is to focus on the concept at the empirical level, recognizing that the linkage between conceptual definition and operational definition is a kind of hypothesis, not a matter for arbitrary assertion. Not all that follows here is fully applicable to every concept.

Univariate research is related to the concept itself rather than its relationship to other concepts (the domain of bivariate research). There is much that is important to know before studying bivariate and multivariate problems. Nonetheless, data about bivariate relationships can be useful in evaluating univariate properties. This section will try to draw a boundary between the univariate and bivariate research uses of bivariate data, but this line exists more in the minds of the researchers—what they are trying to accomplish at a given stage of their work—than in any clear-cut rule.

Unidimensionality

One conceptual issue evoked by the term *univariate* is the question of unidimensionality. Presumably, to this point the reader has been imagining a single attribute, or perhaps a typology created by the intersection of two or three well-defined attributes.

Each single attribute can be operationalized in several ways, and data from these different measures can be combined into an index. Multidimensionality becomes a potential problem for explication when these different measures, each supposedly an indicator of the same latent concept, produce different scores. Is this evidence of several concepts rather than one? Or should these be treated as multiple indicators of a single, unmeasured concept? The decision is a conceptual one, not solvable by empirical methods alone. Whatever decision a researcher makes becomes part of the explication, and is subject to the criteria discussed earlier.

Attitude measurement is one common method beset with problems of unidimensionality (Green, 1954). For example, measures of "attitudes toward the church" could include statements about God, belief systems, church services, ministers, buildings, one's fellow parishioners, membership dues, and many other features that make up the church as an institution in a person's life (Thurstone & Chave, 1929). A given person's favorability score for one of these features may not be the same as that same person's score for other features. If the scores are simply summed across items, two people might have the same score for quite different reasons, which is to say there are different dimensions of evaluation represented in the items. Several paths are open to the investigator in this situation, such as removing items that yield different results from the others; dividing the concept into two or more attributes; or leaving all the items in the scale because they represent different features that explication says belong in a full operational definition. The first two approaches, removing items or dividing the measure into more than one attribute, create unidimensional measures—but they in turn require re-explication to define the new ad hoc concept(s).

Validity is, again, the overarching concern in univariate analyses related to explication, although univariate descriptive studies may have other goals too. Validity is a summary evaluation of the extent to which an operational definition is free from error. As it is often put, does it measure what it is supposed to measure, and only what it is supposed to measure? There are many ways to ask these questions empirically.

Here we will consider first the evaluation of reliability, or freedom from random error. Next we take up validation procedures that go beyond reliability tests to include non-random error as well. We gradually move from intra-concept research, on the variable by itself, to inter-concept research that evaluates the validity of a measure in the context of other variables. This is usually the sequence in which these tasks are undertaken in practice, moving from relatively simple to more complicated assessment procedures.

Evaluating Reliability

As noted earlier, reliability refers to the degree to which an operational definition is free of random error. Assessment of reliability is a major univariate research task and is routinely included in journal articles. Although reliability is a singular concept (as is its complement, random error), there are a number of methods for estimating it, such as test-retest and internal consistency formulas. These methods of estimation are often described as different kinds of reliability because they require different operations and they may yield different estimates. They bear on explication in very similar ways, though, and can be thought of here as different ways of reaching an answer to one question: "How reliable is this measure?" If it is not reliable, it cannot in other respects be of much use; that is, as long as there is an unreliable operational definition, other questions about its validity remain moot. The question of reliability, then, is one the researcher carries along throughout a program of research, constantly adjusting (and, it is hoped, improving) empirical procedures.

Face reliability. It is common to refer to an operation as "valid on its face," but not so common to think of one as "reliable on its face." Still, the first judgmental estimate of reliability is an evaluation of the manifest content of an operational definition. Think first of the ways in which random error ("slippage") might affect the operations a researcher is using to define the concept. The less controlled these extraneous factors, the less reliable a measure will be. A vague question such as, "How important is music to you?" is going to generate a lot more random error than will focused questions like, "Do you own a collection of recorded music?" or "Do you play a musical instrument?"

Assuming that disturbances of each element of an operational definition are random, the principle of multiple operationalism is useful in estimating reliability. Rather than rely on a single indicator, which could be affected by many extraneous influences, the careful researcher might use several parallel indicators. Error that is truly random will tend, across several operations, to cancel itself out. Asking the person the same question at three different times, for example, or asking three fairly similar questions at one time, is likely to be more reliable than merely asking any one question once.

The criterion of specificity (see Chapter 6) is partly in the service of reliability. When a communication researcher relies on people's self-reports, for instance, there is usually less error involved in recalling specific instances (e.g., "Did you talk with your child yesterday?") than in generalizing across many instances (e.g., "How often do you talk with your child?"). The response scale also can make a difference; the more response categories offered—at least up to a point—the less random error will creep into one's data. A dichotomous response scale creates more error than one that makes room for shades of difference—to the extent that such shades exist. Osgood, Suci, and Tannenbaum (1957) tried scales with varying numbers of response categories from 2 to more than 10. They found that reliability improved up to, but not beyond, seven categories; this is why most of their "semantic differential" questionnaires offered exactly seven positions to indicate responses.

To increase face reliability while measuring a finely graded attribute, researchers sometimes break down the respondent's task into simple stages. For example, in assessing a person's party identification in political communication research, the first question may be simply, "General speaking, do you usually think of yourself as a Republican, a Democrat, an independent, or what?" If the person answers "Republican" or "Democrat" there is one follow-up question: "Would you call yourself a strong Republican, or a not very strong Republican?"; if not, a different follow-up question is asked instead: "Do you think of yourself as closer to the Republican or to the Democratic party?" (Question wording taken from Miller & Miller, 1977.)

Other kinds of operational definitions can also be evaluated for reliability on their face. Some communication experiments, for example, involve exposing subjects to different messages. Steps may be taken to maximize reliability of responses to these manipulations, such as repeating the message, or minimizing distractions during laboratory administration, or calling attention to the message. Manipulation checks, which go beyond face reliability of the manipulation, are also used to cull out errant subjects. That is, if the manipulation "didn't take," the case is assumed to be irrelevant to the experimental test of its hypothesized effect, and is discarded as if it represented random error in operationalization.

Test-retest methods. An ambiguous but popular method of assessing reliability of a measure is to remeasure the same people a second time and evaluate the correlations between the two sets of measures. Both true variance and random error, though, contribute to lowering a two-wave test-retest correlation. Unless the concept is an absolutely stable trait within a given person across time, the reliability estimate is depressed not only by true unreliability (random error) but also by true instability of the variable within the people under study. Thus a simple test-retest correlation underestimates the reliability of an operational definition in all cases where there is some possibility for actual instability, too. Methods for estimating stability and reliability separately have been devised for certain situations with more than two time-points of measurement (Heise, 1969; Wiley & Wiley, 1970). If there is instability the correlations farthest apart in time (1-3) tend to be lowest.

Estimating the true stability of a variable over time is a valuable conceptual by-product of this reliability analysis. A concept that does not vary within a group of people across time may be an excellent variable for some research purposes, but it would be a poor selection as a dependent variable in a study where change is hypothesized.

Internal consistency. Another method of estimating reliability is to examine the cross-sectional correlations among several measures of the same variable. This is a common reliability test in communication, where data are gathered in a single administration of a study protocol. The assumption is that, to the extent that different indicators measure the same thing, they should be positively correlated with one another (see unidimensionality, above). Selection of these indicators should emerge from one's explication. The set of correlations can be averaged to yield an estimate of internal consistency such as Cronbach's alpha (Carmines & Zeller, 1979).

A measure should tap the concept in question, but as little else as possible. In survey interviewing especially, though, each question-answer exchange contains what we might call *unique content* that is not shared by the other questions, in addition to the *common content* that presumably represents the concept under study. For example, two questions sometimes used to measure political party identification are, "Which party do you usually vote for?" and "Which party does the most for people like you?" These questions share a lot of common content, but they are not perfectly correlated because some people will vote for the party they think does the best job for the country, rather than for them personally, and some people vote for candidates as individual personalities rather than as an embodiment of party policies. The inter-item correlation is depressed both by random error in tapping the common content, and by systematic error due to the unique content of each item. Internal consistency measures derived from inter-item correlations, then, should be thought of as lower-limit estimates of reliability, even though they represent the average correlation among the items.

Disattenuation for unreliability is a longstanding method of estimating the "true" value of an empirical correlation (McNemar, 1962). Disattenuation is the correction of a raw correlation for random error, which produces higher estimates of a bivariate correlation the lower the estimate of reliability of each measure. Just as test-retest reliability tests may underestimate reliability if they are affected by true instability, internal consistency reliability tests may underestimate reliability if they are affected by unique content of items.

Not all concepts are appropriately measured by highly redundant operational definitions. A researcher's explication may lead to the conclusion that several different kinds of events, perhaps uncorrelated or even negatively correlated, can represent the concept. A "perfect test" would include all these disparate conceptual elements (Selltiz et al., 1964), each tapping an essential, but distinct, aspect of the full concept.

For example, there are several different behaviors that could represent the concept *counterarguing*: open disputes with family or friends, covert thoughts when confronted by persuasive media messages, and so on. A clear explication helps give the scholar confidence in using multiple measures even if these are not correlated. Counterarguing, let us say, means both that someone attempts to persuade a person of something, *and* that the person in turn expresses a contradictory view. Now in day-to-day life, these events are negatively correlated; people in conversation tend to express agreement. But a researcher trying to identify natural occurrences of counterarguing should nevertheless include both these necessary criteria in an operational definition.

Inter-item correlations should not be interpreted mechanically in evaluating a measure. They can be useful, but only in the service of thinking through reliability in relation to other aspects of operationalization. Explication is the basis for such thinking.

Reliability across measures. It is possible for a number of disparate indicators of rather low reliability to produce results that are nevertheless of high reliability. This is a general advantage of multiple indicators. The researcher may combine many error-ridden items into a single index, or conduct a series of studies testing the same proposition with very different kinds of rough indicators.

An example of multi-indicator reliability is a political advertising study by Rothschild (1975). He wanted to compare a series of political issues in terms of their "involvedness," a concept for which he had no direct measure. He tried seven rough indicators, including newspaper coverage, expert ratings, the percentage "undecided" in opinion polls, and his own ratings of poll press releases. He found that classifications of the issues by these different indicators, none of them of obviously high validity for his purpose, agreed 80% of the time. His conclusion was not a technical claim such as, "Inter-item reliability was .80," but rather the working presumption that "data from several weak sources was combined to make stronger determinations." That is, by aligning several rough indicators he arrived at a classification in which he could place considerable research confidence.

How reliable? A frequent question about reliability is how high is high enough? Perfect reliability, which is to say zero random error in operational definitions, is never attained when we are dealing with human communication behavior. But fairly high reliability is especially needed if we are going to evaluate a measure in terms of variance accounted for, or in a measure that is going to be used to classify people for important purposes. For example, intelligence testing, by which students are denied admission to a school or assigned to "fast" versus "slow" academic tracks, demands extremely reliable measurement because the cost of any error could be very high.

If our sample size is large, so that even small correlations should be interpreted as significant—and if we are willing to take seriously a very small correlation—we may be satisfied with somewhat less reliable measures. Looking at it the other way, when we know we are using unreliable variables (e.g., single-item indicators) it makes sense to take seriously any correlation coefficient that reaches statistical significance. This typically occurs at an early stage in data analysis, when we are selecting variables for retention in a model or for incorporation into an index.

Rules of thumb are useful, although not always very sensible. Some writers equate quantitative estimates with evaluations of reliability coefficients, such as .90 = "excellent," .80 = "good," .70 = "satisfactory." These are quite arbitrary, reflecting in part a slavish adherence to the decimal system. High reliability coefficients are easier to achieve with certain kinds of variables, such as content coding, measures based on highly similar items, and highly stable concepts.

Less stringently, we may test the statistical significance of a reliability coefficient. This is not really the way to look at reliability, though, because a significance test merely tells us whether a measure is better than nothing. That is not enough to ask of most operational definitions. What we really want is an estimate of the amount of random error variance in a measure, relative to systematic variance that represents the concept, and nothing else. The researcher should always be making that estimate, and should never be fully satisfied until it has been reduced to as low a value as appears feasible.

Validation

It is impossible to list sufficient criteria for validity; the search for validation continues throughout a program of research. As with reliability, several methods of validation are distinguished, but they are all in the service of one overall judgment.

Face validation. Explication leads to operational definitions that manifestly appear to represent the concept as defined. Some concepts are very close to the operational level (e.g., newspaper reading), while others may be much more abstract and removed (e.g., involvedness). The closer the meaning to the operational definition, the more readily we can accept a claim that a particular measure is "valid on its face." Abstract and operational definitions can converge too much, though; if they were identical there would be no concept other than the operational definition. At most, face validation is only a first-order assessment and may be superseded by better evidence.

Univariate description. Often the empirical properties of a operational definition provide evidence on its validity. For example, if we produce a lot of missing data (e.g., people can't answer the questions), or have difficulty classifying pieces of evidence according to the coding scheme, the measure is probably faulty at least in an operational sense. These problems also hint at low validity at the conceptual level, which means that we need to go back and clarify both the concept and the kinds of evidence we think instantiate it.

Even if we generate a good deal of non-zero and non-equivocal data, the distribution of cases can shed further light regarding validity. For example, if we have thought of the concept as relatively rare, the observed central tendency of the data should be low on the conceptual scale. If most of the cases do not fall into the category we expected, something is probably wrong. We need to rethink the theory behind the concept, or modify the operational procedures.

Variation also tells us something. First, the concept should produce variance, or there may be little to study. I once had the embarrassing experience of asking a sample of nonvoters if their failure to vote had been some sort of protest; not one respondent said it had, so the item was useless for exploring this factor in abstentions. A measure may also produce too much variance, more than we think appropriate for the concept, or the wrong kind of variance. If, for example, we think of the concept as normally distributed, but the empirical distribution turns out to be U-shaped, something may be amiss and we should evaluate the measure for validity in other respects.

Bivariate correlates. Usually the concept explication produces more than one acceptable operational definition, and the researcher should examine the correlations between them. Depending on the research context, this may be viewed as pragmatic, predictive, or concurrent validation.

An example of the use of bivariate correlations in validation comes from a series of studies on children's viewing of violent TV programs. Chaffee (1972) compared answers to the question, "What are your favorite programs?" with measures of "How often do you watch?" several dozen prime-time TV series. The correlation was not very high, casting doubt on the validity of at least one of the measures. In a parallel survey, these children's mothers were also asked to list their child's "favorite programs." This measure turned out to be correlated mostly with the viewing frequency data from the child, not with the latter's own list of "favorite programs." Clearly, these three kinds of questions were not measuring the same attribute of the child's viewing, and the problem was not one of mere inter-item reliability. All three indicators were retained in the analysis for later use, recognizing that they might relate to other concepts in different ways. Correlates need not necessarily represent the same concept to be useful in validation procedures. For example, education is well established (or should be, in the literature review) as a correlate of some communication behaviors. Well-educated people are more likely, for example, to attempt to influence others, to discuss public affairs, to seek information, to read newspapers, and to adopt technological innovations. Measures of any of these concepts, then, should be correlated with education, a variable that is routinely measured in most studies.

Construct validation. Ultimately, a researcher asks not just that an operational definition work in a pragmatic sense, but that it work within an overall theoretical structure, the way the theory predicts. This might be called *theoretical validity*. Not only are the concept's explicated meaning and operationalization evaluated by research testing their relationship, their validity is also enhanced to the extent that they enter into other theoretical relationships that are validated in a larger program of research. Construct validity is the rather demanding term that describes this more extensive, programmatic validation.

In the studies of violence viewing, for example, measures based on the "favorite program" self-report question almost never correlate with aggressive behavior measures, whereas indices built from children's reports of the frequency of actual watching of all available programs are good predictors of aggressiveness (Chaffee, 1972). When the theory at stake is whether viewing TV violence causes aggressiveness, the frequency measure seems more valid than the "favorite program" approach. In another research context, though, such as a study of enjoyment or motives for viewing violent shows, the "favorite program" method might be considered more valid on its face.

Construct validation arises well along in a program of research on a concept, in relation to other concepts. Even a questionable operational definition may, if it enters into a theoretical structure as it should, be considered valid to some extent; a highly reliable measure that nonetheless produces failed hypotheses might not.

Successful validation is far from the end of our efforts. Even though an operation "works" we still may have work to do. For example, McLeod and Chaffee (1972) developed two indices of parent-child communication patterns that consistently predict a wide variety of indicators of adolescent socialization to mass media. These variables survived many tests of hypotheses predicting communication effects in the home, but they did not correlate negatively with one another as the authors had theorized. Construct validity is lacking to the extent that the relationship between the two concepts is not explained theoretically. In this case, the authors reconceptualized family communication patterns as a typology based on two independent dimensions of variation.

Lack of overall construct validation—even when each focal variable by itself seems to work as it should—leaves the researcher in a theoretical quandary. He/she faces the task of ascertaining either what the "successful" operationalization of the concepts contains or lacks, or how the concept or the theory should be changed. Construct validation refers to consistency throughout the theoretical structure, conceptual and operational, including the linking explications. This pursuit may send the researcher back to even the earliest stages of explication.

Summary

Univariate research is the end of this discussion of concept explication, but it is of course not the end of explication itself. The process is cyclical, working back from these stages to earlier ones, as illustrated in Figure 1.1. Univariate research also looks ahead, to bivariate and multivariate studies such as cause-effect analyses. There is a tendency among researchers to hurry past it, to get immediately to these more complex projects. But concepts are the links in a theoretical chain, which can be no stronger. Without careful development of those concepts, and thorough attention to each of them in univariate research, the researcher runs a heightened risk of spending immense time and effort on studies that will amount to very little gain in understanding of human communication.

11. An Example: Age as a Concept

The value of concept explication lies in its use, not as a set of prescriptions but as a series of questions to be considered throughout the research. This final section gives a brief conceptual treatment to age, a variable that is in, but not of, communication research. (While age is not a communication concept itself, focusing on it here underscores the contention that explication is needed wherever we have operational "definitions" that are not tied to conceptual definitions.) Not all the issues raised in this book are relevant to the use of age as a variable in research, but a surprising number are. This section is illustrative. An explication need not be lengthy; its purpose is to help us in other, more extensive, scholarly efforts. If so seemingly simple a measure as age raises significant conceptual questions, this should serve to make the point that more abstract concepts need our thoughtful conceptualization even more.

Age is used as a variable in empirical analyses about as often as is any concept of communication, although it is rarely thought worthy of conceptualization. Age is often entered into causal models (e.g., multiple regression analyses) on a footing equal to conceptualized variables, and in literature reviews it is often used for classification (as an operational contingency). For example, in reviewing the literature on mass media effects for the *Annual Review of Psychology,* Roberts and Bachen (1981) divided all studies into two groups: effects on children and effects on adults. Age is also one of the standard demographic variables that are controlled statistically when statements are offered about communication phenomena. But what is it as a concept?

Primitive terms. To speak of age we need to accept the existence of the person, and of time. This enables us to make such common observations regarding age as "Chuck is 29" or "He's not getting any younger." Preliminary questions of validity rarely arise, unless we suspect someone of lying about his age, as in, "Jack Benny says he is 39." Questions of reliability are not much thought about; age is on its face among the most precise facts to be known about a person.

Preliminary definition. The common language meaning of age might be paraphrased as "the time span between a person's day of birth and his/her most recent birthday." The unit of observation is the individual; the concept varies across persons at any time, and for a single individual across time (at a constant rate of increase). In research the concept is either used as a self-defining quantity, or as a basis for verbal characterization of persons such as "the young" or "middle-aged." These are fuzzily defined categories, referring to several attributes at once; their boundaries in exact terms of years are arguable and differ with differing purposes. But are such age-related terms in common-language use seriously problematic?

Literature search. Even a cursory examination of age in communication research (Chaffee & Wilson, 1975) turns up a good deal of additional employment. Other variables are said to be correlates of age, or "a function of age." These functions are usually assumed to be linear, which means that any increase in age locates a corresponding increase in the other variable. This linear model of age flies in the face of other views—some more literary than scientific perhaps, but nonetheless face-valid too—stressing the curvilinear functions of age. Shakespeare wrote (*As You Like It,* Act II, scene vii) of "seven ages," and was neither the first nor the last to point out similarities between the "mewling and puking" infant and the aged man "sans everything."

While newspapers, for example, usually give people's ages in terms of one-year increments, communication researchers are much less precise. Often they group ages in two or three categories or at best in 10-year blocks. The decimal system, an arbitrary convention, is more related to the number of fingers on our hands than to the number of time units between significant changes in our lives.

Where age is central to one's theory, it is given more thoughtful treatment. Piagetian scholars (e.g., Ward, Wackman, & Wartella, 1977) distinguish between children's information processing capacities at the preoperational, concrete operations, and formal operations stages of development; the child's chronological age is only a rough locator for these concepts.

What, in terms of various communication behaviors and skills, are the significant ages in life? Such a list might include the age of speech (about 2), of reading and writing (about 6), of formal operations (about 11), of regular reading of newspapers (12-15), of peer sharing of music (12-14), of magazine subscription (mid-20s) and so forth. Chaffee and Wilson (1975) found that transitions in several adult media-use habits occur in approximately 8-year segments. An abrupt increase in reading takes place at 65, the standard age for retirement, and after about age 73 Americans become highly dependent upon television (see also Graney, 1975). What is notable here is that few of these boundary ages happen to end in zero. That is, the decade interval is not particularly useful for relating age to communication. It is purely conventional and its standard use as a metric may well produce error.

For some purposes the impact of increasing age decreases with age, so that a log transformation of the raw number of years is the most suitable formal operation. For example, aging up to 40 years produces a considerably greater increase in newspaper readership than does further aging (Chaffee & Choe, 1981). The scale for log(age) is a better representation of the function of age for this predictive purpose than is the equal-interval scale of raw age in years. In child development, too, the effect of one year's growth is not as much during high school as it is in the preschool years.

Empirical description. The expected distribution of age in a general population is no secret; it is skewed to the right, with many more young than old people. In special populations, however, other distributions are possible. In a school student body, for instance, it should be approximately rectangular. Rarely do we find a normal distribution of age, and it is important in statistical analysis to know how a variable deviates from normality.

Descriptive statistics on age are sometimes of interest. If the mean and median are quite different, for example, the distribution is skewed. Some cities are much younger, on the average, than others, and some societies have much greater age variance than others. The role age is expected to play in a theory about communication can be affected by these differences.

Nominal definitions. Age has common noun, verb, and adjectival usages, each potentially a different concept. Noun usages are found among historians ("The Age of Reason"), child-care specialists ("He's going through the Terrible Twos"), and just about everyone else for that matter. Adjectival usages imply variability across persons and need to be kept conceptually distinct from verb usages, which imply variability across time for the same person. There is a difference between saying, "*Older* people are more conservative," and "As people *age*, they become more conservative." The first is a correlational statement about group differences but not necessarily about change. The second is more causal (i.e., more like a theory) and therefore more demanding in terms of evidence. The difference in character between the two statements is perhaps easier to comprehend when thinking about voters. Older people currently vote more conservatively than younger people. But does each person, as an individual, become more conservative as they all age? That is a much more complicated question.

The basic problem is that age is confounded with temporal sequence concepts of all kinds, both personal (development or life cycle) and historical. Neither life cycle development nor history follows a simple monotonic path. Age is not "mere time" because time is rarely "mere"; things happen.

Historical period and cohort usages of age are common too. In recent years much has been written about Baby Boomers, defining a group of people by *an age*, the years in which they were born and reared rather than their current age at any given time. From the end of World War II until the mass dissemination of birth control pills (c. 1962) the birth rate in the United States was much higher than in the previous era (the Great Depression and World War II), or than subsequently. This Baby Boom is an age only in a loose historical aggregate sense. Although those babies are aging, as an age they will be Baby Boomers until they die, and even after. The more nominal definitions we consider, the more problems they raise. Let us take a closer look at what they mean.

Meaning analysis. We have discussed at least four wholly distinct concepts for which the word *age* is used. One is the time span of a person's life to date, in completed years. A second is the verb, to age, meaning to grow older. The third and fourth are the concepts of an era, and of a cohort.

Baby Boomers is an example of a cohort, a term drawn from military operations. In infantry, a military cohort is a row of soldiers who move forward together, perhaps 100 or more abreast, into the fight. Each successive cohort has a different experience of the fray. The first cohort must be exceedingly brave, and few will live to see the result of their valor. Later cohorts may see the tide of battle turn for or against them, but only the later cohorts experience victory or defeat. Analogously, an age cohort marches forward together, through the larger society, from birth to the age of awareness, and on. This common experience, unique to each cohort, shapes its peculiar communication habits along with other features of its social behavior.

The Baby Boom itself, roughly the years 1945-1962, was an era. As an example closer to communication concerns, consider the phrase The Age of Television. Bogart (1958) used this title to call attention to a new era, one in which we still find ourselves. But as a pun one might also let "the age of television" refer to a cohort (assuming that people who have grown up with TV are different from those who have not); to a chronological age (television is at least 50 years old); or to the fact that the TV industry is an aging one, changing quite a bit from what it was in the 1950s.

There are other meanings associated with age that relate to communication too. For example, we often speak of "the age difference" when talking about the relation between two people. Married couples, whatever their exact ages, tend to be quite cognizant of differences of more than a year or two between husband and wife. Age differences are also important to parents in raising their children; some couples space their children well apart in years, but others don't consider a big age difference desirable—at any age—for the kids. This relational concept of age may have important theoretical implications. For instance, a couple may have difficulty communicating because of the age difference. Another relation of potential importance is birth order. In a family, the younger child may develop exceptional speech skills to compensate for the physical disadvantage of competing with a bigger, stronger sibling. Schachter (1959) discovered that first-born and only children behaved differently from later-borns in experiments on affiliation in social settings.

Stripping away the particulars, the meanings of age include references to the number of years that have passed since one's birth, the process of changing as one grows older, a historical era, one's cohort, and a comparison relative to other people. This is in no way an exhaustive list of meanings, but it is sufficient to illustrate the need for some explication.

Empirical definition. Depending upon our research needs, the study of age in relation to communication may require a number of different observations besides the answer to the question, "How old are you?" The research context must be made clear. To study social esteem and deference associated with age, for instance, requires some understanding of cultural values. Age is venerated in a Confucian society, but scorned in some youth-oriented contexts. To evaluate a cohort effect we need to know a good deal about the cultural conditions that obtained during a person's formative years in the particular society where the person lived. To be a Baby Boomer in Butte, say, may not imply becoming a child of the '60s, as it might in Berkeley. To age from 5 to 10 is not the same as aging from 45 to 50, and to have traversed the years 1940 to 1945 is not equivalent to living through the period of 1955 to 1960. To be the younger sister during junior high school is very different from holding that same relative status 20 or 40 years later. Empirical study of age is also a study of contexts, in which age has different meanings.

The minimum required observation poses no deep problem. Everyone who exists can be presumed to have an age, and verbal tools to describe it accurately. The difficulty is that each of us has several ages, or an age in each of a number of senses. Our age refers simultaneously to the time since birth, the cohort that accompanied us, the historical sequence that we alone passed through, the set of age-relations between ourselves and others in our families (our "relations"), and so forth. The sufficient criteria for observing these various ages need to be specified separately for each study.

Aging, a slightly different concept, includes one notable necessity: that the person be alive. Upon death, aging ceases, and age in the sense of time-since-birth becomes frozen; Elvis Presley is forever 42, tops. Some concepts of age, such as birth-order or cohort, do not change prior to death, nor after. The concept of death itself could also be used as an alternative zero-point in place of birth. That is, we could define one's "years of life left" as the functional meaning of age, rather than the more conventional "years of life since birth." In a career, people often count-down their years remaining until retirement.

Mathematical operations on age data are no straightforward matter either. Suppose a group of people, such as a college class or a dinner party, are asked to write down their ages. How should the *mean age*, to take a conventional statistical indicator, be calculated? If you add up the ages and divide by the number of persons in the room, you will get a figure that is approximately 6 months short of the exact value—because each person will normally report his/her age as of the last birthday, which is on the average 6 months in the past.

This simple example leads to consideration of the metric. Should we express our ages to the nearest half-year? The nearest month? Day? Hour? Minute? Each of these has its serious uses, the finer categories being employed mainly near the moment of birth or death. All are arbitrary; we age continuously, not in graded units.

Next, consider scaling. A researcher's cohort, although based on ordinal history, is usually used as a nominal scale. But for most purposes age is at least an ordinal scale. Is it an equal interval scale? It certainly looks like one, and we customarily treat it that way mathematically. But is, say, the difference between the ages of 2 and 10 equal to the difference in ages between 22 and 30, and between 62 and 70? Calculations such as the arithmetic mean assume equal-interval scaling, which means they treat these age spans as equivalent. This may work no mischief in many instances, but it is advisable for a researcher to bear in mind these equal-interval assumptions throughout the entire range of ages every time such calculations are made.

Because age is reported directly in raw numbers that seem on their face to have a zero point, it is common also to treat it as a ratio scale. Even leaving aside the question of whether we should begin counting age at conception rather than at birth, this can introduce problems. Is age 4 "twice" age 2 in the same sense that age 40 is "twice" age 20, or that 60 is "four times" 15? Each of those statements is based on the assumption that age is a ratio scale. Now there may be some situations in which each of these statements makes perfectly good sense, as might be the case when an economist is trying to estimate aggregate food consumption of a population over a considerable period of time. But we might find it hard to defend the statement that a 28-year-old man marrying a 14-year-old woman is "twice her age," especially considering that soon this ratio will no longer hold.

We would not need to delve deeply into the literature on age to note that there are certain natural "fulcrum" ages around which numbers could be calculated as deviations—no matter what the mean of a particular data aggregate. For example, age 21 has important legal and social meanings; so do 18, 65, and some other ages. The life cycle is divided into nonequivalent intervals. Infancy is a discrete period, childhood another, followed by adolescence, adulthood, middle age, retirement, and so on. Each of these is a concept, not just another age, and requires separate explication of its boundaries and its uses in empirical research.

Phases of physical and social change mark the life cycle and bring changes in communication habits. Time spent watching television, for instance, increases steadily throughout childhood; during puberty it begins to decline; and by late adolescence it represents a relatively minor expenditure of a person's time. In adulthood it tends to rise again (Comstock, Chaffee, Katzman, McCombs, & Roberts, 1978).

Evaluative review. Although these thoughts are far from the total picture that a thorough explication of "age as a concept in communication" could bring to light, let us stop and review the definition according to the criteria set forth above.

The degree of specificity in measurement varies depending upon how we intend to use age in our research. Years, or decades, or even the gross dichotomy "under 40" versus "over 40" may suffice in some studies. In other studies, especially of young children, more precise specification of age may be needed.

Reification is not so much of a problem (certainly everyone has, in at least one sense, an age) as is the matter of mistaking a person's age for some other concept. Age is so easily measurable that its various meanings (such as the person's cohort) are easy to forget. A correlational researcher might mistakenly conclude, for example, that age is unrelated to newspaper reading in a broad sample because both young people and old people do not read—but for quite different reasons, the young as a cohort of nonreaders and the old as a result of physical decrepitude.

Consistency of usage is a greater problem than we might at first think when confronted with the everyday word *age*. A person's numerical age is a different matter from the particular effects of growing up or growing old, and related concepts such as birth order and historical cohort need to be disentangled when speaking of "the effects of age" on communication phenomena. None of these concepts is difficult to understand in itself, but the single word is clearly not up to the many tasks to which it might be assigned in empirical research. Clarity in phrasing propositions will always be required to avoid ambiguity. We should not, for example, use the same terminology to refer to "having reached a certain age" and "being the product of another age."

Operational definition. Once the conceptual purpose of age in the research is specified, many of the operational questions fall into line. A few further notes can be useful, though.

Because age has precise, continuous true values, in the common sense of time elapsed since birth, it is an excellent variable to illustrate the problem of sheer unreliability. Even when everyone in a study tells the truth about their ages, there is random error of measurement. This error is greater the less precise our metric; rounding off to the last full year leaves a fair amount of error in the data. In a survey of people who are asked their ages, there is always a distribution of errors (within the range plus or minus 6 months of the exact value). These errors are random because the extent to which they deviate from the true value (minus 6 months) is determined by the day on which they are asked their ages; this date is the same for everyone in the group. Now one can readily imagine that about one-twelfth of any sample of persons will be questioned on a date that is within one month after their last birthday, and another one-twelfth will have a birthday coming in the next month. The sampling distribution of this random error, which is rectangularly distributed, is approximately the same across all samples.

Next, suppose the same sample was remeasured 4 months later. The correlation between their ages at the two times would be less than perfect, because about one-third of them would have aged a year (i.e., they would have celebrated birthdays) while the others would not. Since we know that the true correlation of their ages over time is perfect—the interval between the ages-since-birth of any two members of the sample remain exactly the same over time—this test-retest correlation provides us with an estimate of the reliability of age when it is measured in terms of completed whole years of life. If we measured age in months instead of years this correlation would be higher, which illustrates why finely graded scales tend to be more reliable than coarse scales.

Similarly, if we asked the same people both "What is your age?" and "What year were you born?" the two values would not be perfectly correlated, because of unreliability. Because of the one-year widths of these estimates, there is random error in each; it averages 6 months in each case, but it is a different 6 months. The correlation should be the same for these two measures, taken at the same time, as it would be for either measure alone taken at two different times. This is one variable—perhaps the only one—for which test-retest and multiple-indicators reliability estimates will be the same; they will not be attenuated by either true instability or unique content.

Age is in some ways a uniquely simple variable, albeit an ambiguous word. Most terms of reference used in communication research are a good deal more complex and less palpable. This final section has not, to be sure, dealt with all the potential conceptual issues that might be involved in a thorough explication of age. It should, though, serve to suggest that some explication, in the context of the researcher's particular goals, would be a valuable component of any communication study in which age is a variable.

12. Conclusion

Explication is quite different from other forms of definition. Its purpose is as much to strip away surplus meaning from a term as it is to uncover possible meanings. Whereas a dictionary might offer many meanings, each from a different context, the goal in explication is to center upon one meaning for the particular context in which the researcher is working. The research purpose guides conceptual decisions in parallel fashion at each stage, from analysis of meaning through empirical definition to operational definition. While this book emphasizes the need to refer back at each stage, to compare an evolving operational concept with its intended meaning, there is just as much need to refer forward so that the researcher is developing a conceptual definition that can eventually be worked with operationally.

All of this is clearly denotative. The opposing term *connotative* has two usages, both eschewed in explication. One is the concept of variance in the verbal community, which Skinner (1957) considered the only operationalizable meaning of *connotation*. Invariance of usage is one of the criteria toward which explication works (see Chapter 6). The other, more literary, notion of connotation is that of the many unstated feelings, judgments, and images a term evokes in us. One purpose of meaning analysis (Chapter 5) is to get these elements of a concept out in the open, so we can decide which of them we want to include and which we do not. A term that carries too much baggage may need to be replaced with a less nuanced name for a concept; it is by recognizing these associated meanings that we begin to make such decisions knowingly. If a word or phrase produces the same emotional reaction in everyone, that should be made part of its denotative meaning. Lacking this, the term is ambiguous. After working with it for a time the researcher can decide whether to express some of these personal meanings as part of the concept, or exclude them from the empirical definition.

Explication is an ongoing component of a research program, but it need not at any point be fully represented in a lengthy document. Often the explication section of a published research article is boiled down to one or just a few paragraphs, in which the concept is briefly differentiated from related literature, and its connection to the immediate operational definition is specified. Because explication tells us what to exclude from a definition, much intellectual work may show up as only a few pages of final product. Some of the best explications in original research are among the shortest.

A full explication of a concept, on the other hand, laying out its various usages and their many operational referents, can be a book in itself. The volumes that follow in this series are generally of that character, extensive reviews of the meanings, both historically and in contemporary research contexts, of concepts that have proven themselves useful to the communication field. It is hoped that readers can make use of these monographs as background for further explication in their particular studies, and that this will strengthen the intellectual cohesion of communication as an academic discipline.

References

Allport, G. W. (1955). *Becoming.* New Haven: Yale University Press.

Ball-Rokeach, S. J., & DeFleur, M. L. (1976). A dependency model of mass-media effects. *Communication Research 3,* 3-21.

Bandura, A., Ross, D., & Ross, S. A. (1961). Transmission of aggression through imitation of aggressive models. *Journal of Abnormal & Social Psychology, 63,* 575-582.

Berelson, B. B. (1949). What "missing the newspaper" means. In P. F. Lazarsfeld & F. N. Stanton (Eds.), *Communications research, 1948-1949.* New York: Harper & Bros.

Berelson, B. B., Lazarsfeld, P. F., & McPhee, W. N. (1954). *Voting: A study of opinion formation in a presidential campaign.* Chicago: University of Chicago Press.

Berger, C. R., & Chaffee, S. H. (1987). *Handbook of communication science.* Beverly Hills, CA: Sage.

Berger, P. L., & Luckmann, T. (1972). *The social construction of reality: A treatise in the sociology of knowledge.* Garden City, NY: Doubleday.

Bishop, G. F., Oldendick, R. W., & Tuchfarber, A. J. (1985). The importance of replicating a failure to replicate: Order effects on abortion items. *Public Opinion Quarterly, 49,* 105-114.

Bishop, G. F., Oldendick, R. W., Tuchfarber, A. J., & Bennett, S. E. (1980). Pseudo-opinions on public affairs. *Public Opinion Quarterly, 44,* 198-209.

Blalock, H. M. (1968). The measurement problem: A gap between the languages of theory and research. In H. M. Blalock & A. B. Blalock, *Methodology in social research.* New York: McGraw-Hill.

Blalock, H. M. (1982). *Conceptualization and measurement in the social sciences.* Beverly Hills, CA: Sage.

Blumer, H. (1954). What is wrong with social theory? *American Sociological Review, 19,* 3-10.

Bogart, L. (1958). *The age of television* (2nd Ed.). New York: Ungar.

Brehm, J. W., & Cohen, A. R. (1962). *Explorations in cognitive dissonance.* New York: John Wiley.

Butler, M., & Paisley, W. (1980). *Women and the mass media: Sourcebook for research and action.* New York: Human Sciences Press.

Cantor, M. R., & Pingree, S. (1983). *The soap opera.* Beverly Hills, CA: Sage.

Carmines, E. G., & Zeller, R. A. (1979). *Reliability and validity assessment.* Beverly Hills, CA: Sage.

Carter, R. F. (1962). Stereotyping as a process. *Public Opinion Quarterly, 26,* 77-91.

Carter, R. F. (1965). Communication and affective relations. *Journalism Quarterly, 42,* 203-212.

Carter, R. F., Pyszka, R. H., & Guerrero, J. L. (1969). Dissonance and exposure to aversive information. *Journalism Quarterly, 46,* 37-42.

Chaffee, S. H. (1972). Television and adolescent aggressiveness. In G. A. Comstock & E. A. Rubinstein (Eds.), *Television and social behavior.* Vol. 3. *Tele-*

vision and adolescent aggressiveness (pp. 1-34). Washington, DC: Government Printing Office.

Chaffee, S. H., & Choe, S. Y. (1981). Newspaper reading in longitudinal perspective: Beyond structural constraints. *Journalism Quarterly, 58*, 201-211.

Chaffee, S. H., & Hochheimer, J. L. (1985). The beginnings of political communication research in the United States: Origins of the "limited effects" model. In E. M. Rogers & F. Balle (Eds.), *The media revolution in America and Western Europe* (pp. 267-296). Norwood, NJ: Ablex.

Chaffee, S. H., & Miyo, Y. (1983). Selective exposure and the reinforcement hypothesis: An intergenerational panel study of the 1980 presidential campaign. *Communication Research, 10*, 3-36.

Chaffee, S. H., & Wilson, D. (1975). Adult life cycle changes in mass media use. Paper presented at the meeting of the Association for Education in Journalism, Ottawa, Ontario.

Christians, C. G., & Carey, J. W. (1981). The logic and aims of qualitative research. In G. H. Stempel & B. H. Westley (Eds.), *Research methods in mass communication*. Englewood Cliffs, NJ: Prentice-Hall.

Cohen, A. A., Levy, M. R., & Golden, K. (1988). Children's uses and gratifications of home VCRs: Evolution or revolution. *Communication Research, 15*, 772-780.

Comstock, G., Chaffee, S., Katzman, N., McCombs, M., & Roberts, D. (1978). *Television and human behavior*. New York: Columbia University Press.

Csikszentmihalyi, M., & Kubey, R. (1981). Television and the rest of life: A systematic comparison of subjective experience. *Public Opinion Quarterly, 45*, 317-328.

Deutschmann, P. J., & Danielson, W. A. (1960). Diffusion of knowledge of the major news story. *Journalism Quarterly, 37*, 345-355.

Edwards, A. L. (1957). *Techniques of attitude scale construction*. New York: Appleton-Century-Crofts.

Elguea, J. (1984). Sociology of development and philosophy of science: A case study in contemporary scientific growth. Unpublished doctoral dissertation, Stanford University.

Festinger, L. (1957). *A theory of cognitive dissonance*. Palo Alto, CA: Stanford University Press.

Festinger, L. (1964). *Conflict, decision and dissonance*. Palo Alto, CA: Stanford University Press.

Gerbner, G., Gross, L., Morgan, M., & Signorielli, N. (1980). The "mainstreaming" of America: Violence profile No. 11. *Journal of Communication, 30, (3)*, 10-29.

Graney, M. (1975). Communication uses and the social activity constant. *Communication Research, 2*, 347-366.

Green, B. F. (1954). Attitude measurement. In G. Lindzey (Ed.), *Handbook of social psychology* (pp. 335-369). Cambridge, MA: Addison-Wesley.

Hage, J. (1972). *Techniques and problems of theory construction in sociology*. New York: John Wiley.

Heider, F. (1959). *The psychology of interpersonal relations*. New York: John Wiley.

Heise, D. R. (1969). Separating reliability and stability in test-retest correlation. *American Sociological Review, 34*, 93-101.

Hempel, C. G. (1952). *Fundamentals of concept formation in empirical science*. Chicago: University of Chicago Press.

Herzog, H. (1944). What do we really know about daytime serial listeners? In P. F. Lazarsfeld & F. N. Stanton (Eds.), *Radio research 1942-1943*. New York: Duell, Sloan & Pearce.

76

Hovland, C. I. (1959). Reconciling conflicting results from experimental and survey studies of attitude change. *American Psychologist, 14*, 8-17.

Hovland, C. I., Lumsdaine, A. A., & Sheffield, F. D. (1949). *Experiments on mass communication.* Princeton, NJ: Princeton University Press.

Iyengar, S. (1987). Television news and citizens' explanations of national affairs. *American Political Science Review, 81*, 815-831.

Jacoby, J. (1975). Perspectives on a consumer information processing research program. *Communication Research, 2*, 203-215.

Katz, E., & Feldman, J. J. (1962). The debates in the light of research: A survey of surveys. In S. Kraus (Ed.), *The great debates.* Bloomington: Indiana University Press.

Katz, E., & Lazarsfeld, P. F. (1955). *Personal influence.* New York: Free Press.

Klapper, J. T. (1960). *The effects of mass communication.* New York: Free Press.

Krugman, H. E. (1965). The impact of television advertising: Learning without involvement. *Public Opinion Quarterly, 29*, 349-356.

Kuhn, T. S. (1970). *The structure of scientific revolutions* (2nd Ed.). Chicago: University of Chicago Press.

Lazarsfeld, P. F., Berelson, B., & Gaudet, H. (1944). *The people's choice.* New York: Columbia University Press.

MacCorquodale, K., & Meehl, P. (1948). On a distinction between hypothetical constructs and intervening variables. *Psychology Review, 55*, 95-107.

Machlup, F. (1962). *The production and distribution of knowledge in the United States.* Princeton, NJ: Princeton University Press.

Martin, R. R., McNelly, J. T., & Izcaray, F. (1976). Is media exposure unidimensional? A socioeconomic approach. *Journalism Quarterly, 53*, 619-625.

Marx, K. (1867). Capital. Ed. by F. Engels. London: Swan Sonnenschein, Lowry & Co.

McLeod, J. M., & Chaffee, S. (1972). The construction of social reality. In J. Tedeschi (Ed.), *The social influence processes* (pp. 50-99). Chicago: Aldine-Atherton.

McLeod, J. M., & McDonald, D. (1985). Beyond simple exposure: Media orientations and their impact on political processes. *Communication Research, 10*, 155-174.

McLuhan, M. (1964). *Understanding media: The extensions of man.* New York: McGraw-Hill.

McNemar, Q. (1962). *Psychological statistics, 3rd. Ed.* New York: John Wiley.

Miller, W. E., & Miller, A. H. (1977). *The CPS 1976 American national election study: Pre- and post-election waves. Vol. 1.* Ann Arbor: University of Michigan Center for Political Studies.

Monge, P. R. (1990). Theoretical and analytical issues in studying organizational processes. *Organization Science, 1*, 406-430.

Osgood, C. E., Suci, G. J., & Tannenbaum, P. H. (1957). *The measurement of meaning.* Urbana: University of Illinois Press.

Palmer, E. (1981). Shaping persuasive messages with formative research. In R. E. Rice & W. J. Paisley (Eds.), *Public communication campaigns* (pp. 227-238). Beverly Hills, CA: Sage.

Parker, E. B. (1963). The effects of television on magazine and newspaper reading: A problem in methodology. *Public Opinion Quarterly, 27*, 315-320.

Payne, S. (1951). *The art of asking questions.* Princeton, NJ: Princeton University Press.

Ray, M. L. (1973). Marketing communication and the hierarchy-of-effects. In P. Clarke (Ed.), *New models for communication research* (pp. 147-176). Beverly Hills, CA: Sage.

77

Reeves, B. (1989). Theories about news and theories about cognition: Arguments for a more radical separation. *American Behavioral Scientist, 33,* 191-198.

Reeves, B., Thorson, E., & Schleuder, J. (1986). Attention to television: Psychological theories and chronometric measures. In J. Bryant & D. Zillmann (Eds.), *Perspectives on media effects.* Hillsdale, NJ: Lawrence Erlbaum.

Ritchie, D., Price, V., & Roberts, D. F. (1987). Television, reading, and reading achievement. *Communication Research, 14,* 292-315.

Ritchie, L. D. (1991). *Communication concepts 2: Information.* Newbury Park, CA: Sage.

Roberts, D. F., & Bachen, C. M. (1981). Mass communication effects. *Annual Review of Psychology, 32,* 307-356.

Rogers, E. M. (1964). *Diffusion of innovations.* New York: Free Press.

Rogers, E. M. (1976). Communication and development: The passing of the dominant paradigm. *Communication Research, 3,* 213-240.

Rogers, E. M. (1983). *Diffusion of innovations, 3rd Ed.* New York: Free Press.

Rogosa, D., Brandt, D., & Zimowski, M. (1982). A growth curve approach to the measurement of change. *Psychological Bulletin, 92,* 729-748.

Roser, C. (1990). Involvement, attention, and perceptions of message relevance in the response to persuasive appeals. *Communication Research, 17,* 571-600.

Rothenbuhler, E. W. (1988). The living room celebration of the Olympic Games. *Journal of Communication, 38(4),* 61-81.

Rothschild, M. L. (1975). On the use of multiple methods and multiple situations in political communications research. In S. H. Chaffee (Ed.), *Political communication: Issues and strategies for research.* Beverly Hills, CA: Sage.

Salmon, C. T. (1986). Perspectives on involvement in consumer and communication research. In B. Dervin & M. Voigt (Eds.), *Progress in communication sciences.* Norwood, NJ: Ablex.

Schachter, S. (1959). *The psychology of affiliation: Experimental studies of the sources of gregariousness.* Palo Alto, CA: Stanford University Press.

Schramm, W. (1949). The nature of news. *Journalism Quarterly, 26,* 259-269.

Schramm, W. (1963). *The science of human communication.* New York: Basic Books.

Schramm, W., Lyle, J., & Parker, E. B. (1961). *Television in the lives of our children.* Palo Alto, CA: Stanford University Press.

Schuman, H., Presser, S., & Ludwig, J. (1981). Context effects on survey responses to questions about abortion. *Public Opinion Quarterly, 45,* 216-223.

Sears, D. O., & Chaffee, S. H. (1979). Uses and effects of the debates: An overview of empirical studies. In S. Kraus (Ed.), *The great debates: Ford vs. Carter, 1976.* Bloomington: Indiana University Press.

Sears, D. O., & Freedman, J. L. (1967). Selective exposure to information: A critical review. *Public Opinion Quarterly, 31,* 194-213.

Selltiz, C., Jahoda, M., Deutsch, M., & Cook, S. W. (1964). *Research methods in social relations* (revised one-volume edition). New York: Holt, Rinehart & Winston.

Shannon, C. (1949). The mathematical theory of communication. In C. Shannon & W. Weaver, *The mathematical theory of communication.* Urbana: University of Illinois Press.

Skinner, B. F. (1957). *Verbal behavior.* New York: Appleton-Century-Crofts.

Stevens, S. S. (1946). On the theory of scales of measurement. *Science, 103,* 677-680.

78

Thurstone, L. L., & Chave, E. J. (1929). *The measurement of attitude.* Chicago: University of Chicago Press.
Tichenor, P. J., Donohue, G. A., & Olien, C. N. (1970). Mass media and differential growth in knowledge. *Public Opinion Quarterly, 34,* 158-170.
Ward, S., Wackman, D. B., & Wartella, E. (1977). *How children learn to buy.* Beverly Hills, CA: Sage.
Webb, E. J., Campbell, D. T., Schwartz, R. D., & Sechrest, L. (1966). *Unobtrusive measures: Nonreactive research in the social sciences.* Chicago: Rand McNally.
Wiley, D. E., & Wiley, J. A. (1970). The estimation of measurement error in panel data. *American Sociological Review, 35,* 112-117.

Author Index

Allport, G. W., 9

Bachen, C. M., 63
Ball-Rokeach, S. J., 27
Bandura, A., 45
Bennett, S. E., 45
Berelson, B. B., 11, 20, 46
Berger, C. R., 26, 29
Berger, P. L., 26, 29
Bishop, G. F., 40, 45
Blalock, H. M., 6, 30
Blumer, H., 41
Bogart, L., 67
Brandt, D., 17
Brehm, J. W., 30
Butler, M., 35

Campbell, D. T., 46
Cantor, M. R., 47
Carey, J. W., 41
Carmines, E. G., 56
Carter, R. F., 9, 22, 26
Chaffee, S. H., 17, 20-21, 26, 29, 49,
    60-61, 64-65, 70
Chave, E. J., 37, 39, 52
Choe, S. Y., 17, 65
Christians, C. G., 41
Cohen, A. A., 30, 47
Cohen, A. R., 30, 47
Comstock, G., 70
Cook, S. W., 14
Csikszentmihalyi, M., 45

Danielson, W. A., 23
DeFleur, M. L., 27

Deutsch, M., 14, 23
Deutschmann, P. J., 23
Donohue, G. A., 3, 41

Edwards, A. L., 37, 39
Elguea, J., 27

Feldman, J. J., 20
Festinger, L., 30
Freedman, J. L., 21

Gaudet, H., 11, 20
Gerbner, G., 12
Golden, K., 47
Graney, M., 64
Green, B. F., 39, 52
Gross, L., 12, 27
Guerrero, J. L., 22

Hage, J., 10, 15
Heider, F., 10
Heise, D. R., 55
Hempel, C. G., 7, 24, 29
Herzog, H., 47
Hochheimer, J. L., 21
Hovland, C. I., 11, 19

Iyengar, S., 40
Izcaray, F., 23

Jacoby, J., 9
Jahoda, M., 14

About the Author

Steven H. Chaffee (Ph.D., Stanford University, 1965) is Janet M. Peck Professor of International Communication at Stanford University. He has published six dozen articles, books, and chapters on research in the areas of mass media effects, political socialization, voter behavior, family communication, co-orientation, international communication, and research methods. His books include *Using the Mass Media* (with Michael Petrick), *Political Communication* (editor), *Television and Human Behavior* (with George Comstock and others), and *Handbook of Communication Science* (co-edited with Charles Berger). He has served as editor of *Communication Research: An International Quarterly* and on the editorial boards of seven other journals and series. A former newspaper reporter and editor, he was Vilas Research Professor in the School of Journalism and Mass Communication at the University of Wisconsin-Madison, and has also taught at the University of California, Berkeley; the University of California, Los Angeles; and the University of Michigan.

NOTES